Also by Matthew Kelly

The Rhythm of Life
The Seven Levels of Intimacy
Perfectly Yourself
The Dream Manager

Building Better Families

Matthew Kelly

Building
Better
Families

A Practical Guide to Raising Amazing Children

BALLANTINE BOOKS | NEW YORK

Published in the United States by Ballantine Books,
an imprint of The Random House Publishing Group,
a division of Random House, Inc., New York.

Ballantine and colophon are registered trademarks
of Random House, Inc.

LIBRARY OF CONGRESS CATALOGING-IN-PUBLICATION DATA

Kelly, Matthew.
    Building better families : a practical guide to raising
amazing children / Matthew Kelly.
        p.   cm.
    ISBN 978-0-345-49453-5 (hardcover)
1. Family.   2. Parenting.   3. Child rearing.   I. Title.
HQ734.K374 2008
646.7'8—dc22   2007032389

Printed in the United States of America on acid-free paper

www.ballantinebooks.com

9 8 7 6 5 4 3 2 1

First Edition

Book design by Mary A. Wirth

Contents

Introduction

I was in Philadelphia recently presenting a series of seminars when I had an inspiring encounter with one of my readers. During the course of the weekend I met with many of the attendees, but it was the story of one woman that touched me deeply. For many years she had been reading my work and applying the message to her own life, but had always wondered how as a single mother she could use the message to inspire her young son. This is the story she told me.

"Then one night, I was putting him to bed and I asked him a question that I had been asking myself for years. 'What did you do today to become a-better-version-of-yourself physically, emotionally, intellectually, and spiritually?' He was only seven years old, and he just looked at me strangely. The question had taken him by surprise. But the next night as I was putting him to bed he asked, 'Don't you want to know what I did today to become a-better-version-of-myself?' We went through each of the four areas and he told me how he had tried to improve that day physically, emotionally, intellectually, and spiritually. It was one of those moments that touches you at your very core. My son is eleven now and for almost four years, every night, we have discussed the same question. I see him growing into such a fine, thoughtful, intelligent, and generous young man, and I know that it would not be quite like this if it were not for that question . . . and that habit. As a single mom I don't have anywhere near as much time as I would like to for parenting, but I do what I can. It's amazing how one small but central message, and habit, has changed our relationship, and our lives."

I hope you find one new life-changing parenting habit in these pages also.

After *The Seven Levels of Intimacy* was published, I did a media tour to discuss the ideas in the book with interviewers and readers. I still remember the first interview, a local television morning news program. The interviewer began by asking me if I was married. I explained that I was not. The interviewer then proceeded to ask me how I could write about intimacy, in essence questioning my eligibility or qualifications to write on the subject.

This line of questioning repeated itself over and over again, interview after interview, in the following weeks and months, and even to this day, I receive e-mails from readers asking the same sorts of questions.

My answer in that first interview was to smile, because I enjoy the challenge, and say, "Just because someone is a great football player that does not qualify them as a great football coach. In fact, many of the greatest coaches in history had little or no ability to speak of as players. . . ."

You don't have to be a great player, to be a great coach. Experience is not the only teacher. If it were, we would not read books.

So, now I tackle the subject of family. I am not married and I have no children, so some people may consider me to be on the sideline of life in these things. But from the sidelines, we see things that the players in the game cannot see, either because they are too close to the action to gain perspective, or because the game is moving too quickly about them.

Perhaps more important, in the course of my work and travels, married men and women have come to me as mothers and fathers and as husbands and wives. They have confided in me, shared their triumphs and trials, and sought counsel. These pages are filled with all I have learned from them and their situations. I hope you find them helpful. If you discover within these pages self-evident truths that you can confirm with your everyday experience of life and people, embrace them and apply them to your life! If not, set them aside and move forward. I wish you well in your journey.

Building Better Families

1

The Changing Face of Families

It has been only fifteen years since I graduated from high school, but the world has changed at warp speed during that time. Those changes are no more apparent than in the area of family. More than 50 percent of America's children now live separated from their biological fathers. Like many, I think this is tragic, but I do not want to write a book about that tragedy. There has been enough written already. We can sit around cursing the darkness or we can turn on the light and find the best path forward.

What Is a Family?

It's an interesting question. If you want to have some heated conversation, get a diverse group of people together for a dinner party and raise this question. This topic is nothing short of explosive at this time, both socially and politically.

There are many who would say the answer is very simple. A family is a mother and a father and their children. This answer is usually announced with a tone of absolute certainty, sometimes even arrogance, as if it were as obvious as the day is long and as old as time itself. Though if we travel across the Atlantic Ocean to Europe or south of the border to Central and South America, we quickly discover that a multigenerational definition of family that includes not only parents and children but grandparents and great grandparents is very much alive and well in many cultures. These cultures are also very much in celebration of the intergenerational definition of family that includes aunts and uncles, cousins, and nieces and nephews.

The same person who answered with all that certainty— "A family is a mother and a father and their children."— would reply to these points by saying, "Well, of course we consider grandparents, aunts, uncles, cousins, nieces, and nephews to be part of a family in a broader sense." You see, in America today, the question—What is a family?—has become a secret code for the political question: Who should raise children?

I have had the pleasure of watching my good friend Pat Lencioni, the famed business author and consultant, work with executive teams on a couple of occasions. One of the exercises he does with these executives concerns the idea of core values. Most business leaders would now agree that a company should have a set of core values. If you were to visit the head office of most companies, you'd discover that these core values appear in various places—from annual reports to plaques in lobbies to mini-posters in hallways, cubicles, and lunchrooms. But if you ask most employees what do these core values mean, they will tell you that they mean nothing. This is because of how they were arrived at. A group of executives got together one day and decided they needed some core values for the company because they saw that some other company had them, and besides, it is now accepted wisdom that all companies should have stated core values. They pick values like integrity, compassion, and service. But the employees know from their everyday experience that these core values do not exist, and so rather than creating unity, they create disengagement and resentment.

The problem is that when the executive team sits down to arrive at their core values, they don't ask: What are our core values? Rather, they ask: What should our core values be? So, what they come up with are in fact aspirational values (what they want the values of the company to be) not actual core values (what the values of the company actually are at this very moment).

Similarly, when the question is raised—What is a family?—most people reply by describing what they think the ideal family should be and not by describing their actual family, or the reality of most families.

Returning then to the dinner party reply—"A family is a mother and a father and their children."—let's have a look at how many people this definition excludes. Certainly a gay couple raising a child is excluded, and this, of course, is exactly who this answer is designed to exclude more often than not. But if we move for a moment beyond this highly emotionally charged social and political issue, who else gets excluded by this definition of family? Single mothers and their children, couples who are unable to have children, adopted children, foster families, grandparents raising children and the children being raised by grandparents, husbands and wives in second marriages and the children they are raising from either marriage, and so on.

If the question were: What is the best situation in which a child should be raised? I would tell you that in my own opinion the best scenario would be for a child to be raised by a loving biological mother and father who are deeply in love with each other, permanently committed to their own and to each other's growth, and to supporting their child to become all he or she was created to be and achieve all he or she was created to accomplish. I would probably also add broad and deep intergenerational and multigenerational aspects to their family life along with the best education, opportunities to travel, and on and on and on.

That would be perfect, but in reality the life of human beings cannot be neatly packaged. Life tends to be messy most of the time. Very few children have these circumstances in all their breadth and depth, perhaps none. Though it does help to know what perfect would look like.

But the question is: What is a family? A family is not what we think a family should be, or what we hope to have, or should have, or what would be ideal—a family is what we actually have. A family is the one we've got. None of them perfect and all of them messy from time to time. Some of them messier than others. But there is no point telling someone that what they have is not a family.

So, while it is critically important that we continue to recognize and celebrate the ideal for a family and the ideal for raising children, it is more important that we realize where we are and what we have to work with—and begin that work today. In the pages that follow, you will find tools and insights to help you in the work of building a better family. The title is not Building Perfect Families. Perfect families exist only in our minds, and it is these imaginings that are very often the enemy of our ability to enjoy the wonderful family we already have, or might have if we made it just that little bit more of a priority.

Family and Today's Culture—Opposing Purposes

The only place to begin our discussion of building better families is with an examination of purpose. What is the purpose of a family? The answer to this question can only be drawn from a vision of a human person. People do not exist for families; families exist for people. What, essentially, is a person's purpose? If you have read any of my earlier works you know that I have repeatedly proposed that our essential purpose is to become the-best-version-of-ourselves. You are here to become all you were created to be. You are not here exclusively to do something or accomplish certain tasks, but to be and become someone. All the doing that fills our lives— relationships, school, work, politics, community involvement, recreation—is designed simply to provide opportunities for us to become the-best-version-of-ourselves. Could you have any better dream for your children, your spouse, or your parents than for them to truly become and fully celebrate the-best-version-of-themselves? It is the ultimate dream for those we love.

Our vision for family springs from this vision for a person. So we ask the question again: What is the purpose of a family? The purpose of a family is to help one another become the-best-version-of-ourselves and in the process contribute to the greater good of society and humanity. The family is the building block of all great societies. Sadly, we don't hear much about the building of great societies anymore, and that may be because we mistakenly believe we already have them. So, though it should be unnecessary to ask the question, for the sake of clarity: Why is it important to build and sustain great societies? Because great societies give rise to great men and women who celebrate their best selves and in turn raise humanity to new levels. A family (or a culture or a society, for that matter) is not an end in itself, but exists at the service of a greater purpose. Families, cultures, and societies are true to themselves when they help their members become better-versions-of-themselves.

On paper this may all make sense, but you and I know how difficult it is to celebrate and defend our best self in the moments of everyday living, even before we take into account the influence of our environments.

People and families live in the midst of societies and cultures. In a utopian world, everything about a culture would be aimed toward helping each member of society become the-best-version-of-himself or -herself. In our very human world, however, we know this is not so. It is therefore important to examine the motives of the culture in which we live.

What is the purpose of culture? In general, the role of culture is to offer a broadening experience for the people of a society. But even this broadening should serve some greater overall purpose. Broadening simply for the sake of broadening is dangerous, irresponsible, and reckless. In its truest expression, culture would expose people to a broadening set of ideas and experiences that would be aimed at inspiring and assisting each member of that society to become a-better-version-of-themselves. Every aspect of the human experience should be seen with our essential purpose in mind. Culture is therefore only valuable to the extent that it helps the members of a society celebrate their best selves.

It is needless to say, and blatantly obvious, that our modern culture fails to deliver in this regard in too many ways to list. At every turn we are assaulted by ideas and experiences that not only do not assist us in our quest to become the-best-version-of-ourselves, but even worse, often introduce obstacles that significantly prevent us from embracing our best selves and following our destinies. Music, movies, television, magazines, theater, a visit to the mall, concerts . . . it has become increasingly rare that we emerge from any of these inspired to become a-better-version-of-ourselves.

So, what exactly is our culture trying to achieve? This is where we stumble upon the alarming truth. The vision of our culture is a nonvision. The agenda of our culture is a non-agenda. Our culture is not so much the presence of something as it is the absence of something. The stark reality is that our culture does not have a vision for the human person.

If that sounds a little confusing, imagine how confusing the actual experience of such a culture is for the average teenager.

We inevitably arrive at this haunting question: If there is no grand vision or agenda for our culture, what is driving it? You know the answer. Think for a moment. What is driving the modern popular culture in which our society is immersed? The answer: advertising and consumption. The goal of much of what drives our culture today seems to be nothing more than to create and encourage consumption. Last year's clothes, though there is nothing wrong with them and they remain as perfectly *useful* as they were last year, are now magically no good, even inadequate, because they are out of fashion. The same is true of cars, cell phones, furniture, electronics, and hundreds of other items in dozens of other categories.

The practical reality is that the modern culture does not elevate a person; it consumes a person. The purpose of the family and the nonpurpose of the present culture are therefore directly opposed to each other. This places the family right at the heart of a cultural war.

Cultural War

Anyone interested in becoming the-best-version-of-himself or -herself has an uphill battle in today's culture. It is true that this desire to become all we are capable of being would be difficult even in a culture that attempted to help people in this quest. The internal obstacles—laziness, procrastination, addiction—make it difficult enough as we strive to fulfill our destiny. A culture that opposes our quest adds a whole different set of challenges.

The greatest problem is not that the culture is what it is, but rather that we do not see it for what it is. That the culture opposes our efforts to become our best selves is a problem, but the greater problem is that we do not recognize or actively acknowledge that the culture opposes our essential purpose.

The consequence of these opposing purposes is that whether you are aware of it or not, if you are trying to achieve any of the following, you are in the middle of a cultural war:

- Build a better family
- Raise amazing children
- Have a great marriage
- Become the-best-version-of-yourself

Our present culture does not lend itself to building better families, it promotes the destruction of families. This makes sense, if consumption is at the heart of our culture's non-vision, because a broken family needs two of everything—two houses, two washing machines, two lawn mowers, two kitchen tables, and so on. If to create and perpetually increase consumption was your goal, you would want every family in the world to be broken apart as much as possible.

Similarly, our culture does not lend itself to raising amazing children. When was the last time you saw a really well-adjusted, selfless, thoughtful, child or teenager at the center of a popular television show? What place does our modern culture have for the compassion and virtue of a young person like Anne Frank?

If one of your goals was to have a really dynamic and wonderful marriage, and if you could choose between a variety of cultures, you certainly wouldn't pick today's. This culture's ability to promote and sustain healthy marriages is now beyond a joke. In fact, what, if anything, does our culture do to promote dynamic and faithful marriage?

And finally, the big picture, in how many ways does our culture help you become the-best-version-of-yourself? Very few. Someone who seriously wants to grow in the midst of this culture is required to make a very concerted effort, to seek out the resources necessary to nurture such a journey, and to steel themselves against the never-ending onslaught of ideas and images that constantly present themselves and try to lure you away from your path. Why? No real reason, no real vision, no great agenda other than to sell you something (ideas or products). And again, we discover that consumption is not driven by the self-assured individual dedicated to being a well-rounded healthy contributing member of society. No, consumption is driven by the self-centered, self-interested, pleasure-seeking, insecure soul who needs the latest of everything in order to feel that he or she has any real worth. An emotionally healthy person consumes less than an emotionally unhealthy person. That's why so much advertising does not make you feel good about yourself and the contribution you can make to society, but rather creates insecure and needy consumers who think that buying and having will deliver them to a place where they are at peace with themselves.

With every passing day, our culture caters more and more to the lowest common denominator. In doing so, the great center of society continues to be dragged to lower levels. The-least-possible-version-of-ourselves is where the culture is leading us. If you are the slightest bit interested in building a better family, raising amazing children, having a great marriage, and becoming the-best-version-of-yourself, it is time to recognize and daily affirm that the culture is not your friend. You are, in fact, in the middle of a very serious cultural war.

Still not convinced that our culture is in crisis? Here are some of the signs. There are more than 2.2 million people in America's prisons and jails, another 4 million on probation, and almost another million on parole. It is estimated that

80 percent of these have substance dependencies. In 2005, there were 16,692 murders committed in the United States. During that same year, 93,934 rapes were reported, and the great majority of sexual assaults continue to go unreported. The annual incidence of domestic violence is greater than a million cases, and pregnant woman have increasingly become the target of such attacks. In 2002, Americans reported over 159 million alcohol-impaired driving trips. More than one million drivers are arrested each year under the influence of alcohol or narcotics. Every day 8,000 teens become infected with a new sexually transmitted disease. More than 50 percent of fifteen-year-old girls have had oral sex. Every seven seconds a teenage girl becomes addicted to smoking. Sixty-five percent of sixteen-year-old males view pornography at least once every ten days. The suicide rate among young adults and teens has increased 5,000 percent over the last five decades. Depression has reached epidemic levels. College life is celebrated as four years of excessive drunkenness, sexual promiscuity, general recklessness, and disregard for others, to the point that if you do not participate you are looked upon as if there is something wrong with you.

Dr. Peter Kreeft, professor of philosophy at Boston College and author of more than twenty-five books, explained it in this way: "If you can't see that our entire civilization is in crisis, then you are a wounded victim of the war. We are now engaged in the most serious war that the world has ever known. To win any war, the three most necessary things to know are (1) that you *are* at war, (2) who your enemy is, (3) what weapons or strategies can defeat that enemy. You cannot win a war (1) if you simply sow peace on a battlefield,

(2) if you fight civil wars against your allies, or (3) if you use the wrong weapons."

I would add that it is critically important to know what you are fighting for, what you are defending, why it is important to win, and what is at stake if you lose—and that it is also vital that you know who your allies are. Knowledge of these is what gives courage and resolve to our hearts in times of testing.

Not only does today's culture present an opposing purpose, but it is a real force to be reckoned with. If we are serious about building better families, it would serve us well to recognize at the outset that a little tweaking here and there is probably not going to get the job done. It is also important to realize that no technique (including those I will share with you in chapters three and four of this book) sprinkled here and there, in and of itself, is enough to win this cultural war and build better families. What is needed is a strategy, a life-giving strategy, that can be applied over and over again to the moments of our everyday lives.

Are You Willing?

The most cursory and elementary examination of our culture along the lines of the hopes and dreams we have for our families quickly reveals that our current culture and any authentic vision of family are massively at odds with each other. But what are we willing to do about it?

Most parents say they would do whatever was necessary to help their child grow free and strong and succeed. But are you willing to be countercultural? This is the question it all hangs upon.

By being countercultural I mean being willing to step away from the culture whenever it does not help you and your family to become a-better-version-of-yourselves. People who are countercultural are often ridiculed. This can be difficult, but it can also be clarifying and can help both children and parents to develop character. And the truth is, if enough people choose a countercultural lifestyle, they will create a new culture. That is the only way a new culture will be born. If enough people stop going to movies that are filled with violence and foul language, the powers that be will start making more movies that support you in your quest to become your best self. This is true across all industries. The markets will go where there is demand.

It is abundantly clear what the fruits of our current culture are. We must decide if this is what we want for our children, our families, and ourselves. If we want a different result, then we must take a different approach. If we want a *radically* different result, and my experience has been that most parents do, then we need a *radically* different approach. And I assure you, this will require more courage and inner fortitude on the part of parents than it will from our children. It is hard to be a leader, and make no mistake, your role as a parent is a leadership role.

In my own life, whenever I set out to accomplish something, I look around to find out who has done it before and what has made them successful. When it comes to raising children, I don't know anyone who has done a better job than my friends Mark and Liz in Louisville, Kentucky. They have two daughters, Katie and Lisa. Now just twenty-three and nineteen, they are mature, generous, thoughtful, fun-loving, and genuinely kind young women. I am confident you could put Katie and Lisa in a room with anyone—from heads of state to the homeless—and they would conduct themselves in a way that would impress, and quite possibly amaze. They are the most well-adjusted, contributing, intelligent, engaging young ladies I know.

Do they get on each other's nerves from time to time? Sure. Are they strikingly similar at the core and yet incredibly unique in other ways? No question. Did Mark and Liz win the parenting lottery? Absolutely not.

Luck has nothing to do with the results their parenting has achieved. As I have observed them throughout our friendship of almost a decade now, there are a thousand things I see Mark and Liz doing on a regular basis that make them great parents. At the same time, I think their success can be summarized in two words: involved and interested. They are genuinely interested in their children's journeys—their hopes and dreams, fears and failures, questions and needs. They also genuinely enjoy being involved in their daughters' lives. It is not something they have to do; it is something they get to do. They see it as the privilege of a lifetime, not something to be squeezed into the schedule.

But Mark and Liz's success as parents also springs from a myriad of personal habits. In the first place, they are both dedicated to continuous learning and to their own personal growth. They can make the most routine experience into an adventure. They are genuinely interested in other people, even if they have just met them. They live simply and well within their means. They are both avid readers. They are willing to make sacrifices for each other, for their children, and for their friends. Interestingly enough, these habits are for the most part countercultural.

I remember when it was time for Lisa to start driving. She practiced driving and passed her exam and was told her parents would give her $15,000 to buy her first car. At the time Mark was the CEO of a company with more than six billion dollars' worth of annual revenue, and his own compensation was in the millions. He certainly could have afforded to buy his daughter any car she wanted. But Mark and Liz live in a modest home, they drive American cars, and have made a conscious decision to live the way they do. Mark and Lisa spent weeks talking about cars, looking through the papers at used cars, and finally Lisa decided upon a blue Oldsmobile SUV. Giving her a budget helped her understand that money is a finite commodity, and now that she has her car, she has to pay for gas with her own money from babysitting and her summer job.

It would have been easier for Mark and Liz to lease her a brand-new Jetta, bring it home, and be done with it. But how many lessons would Lisa have missed out on? Not only that, for the rest of her life Lisa will look back on the experience of buying her first car and have great memories of an experience with her parents.

By the time the average American child is six years old she will have spent more time watching television than she will spend speaking to her father in her entire life. This is certainly not true for Katie and Lisa, and not because they have not watched their fair share of television. But because both Mark and Liz have made the ultimate investment in their children—time. Young people yearn for time with their parents. Time to know and be known. Time to mess around, and enough time that the kidding around can create the ease necessary to talk about more serious things.

This is an example of successful parenting and a fine family. Are they perfect? Of course not, and they would be the first to tell you that. But there is great success here. As parents, as children, as spouses, as siblings, they are doing something right . . . and something worthy of our emulation. And if you look closely, I think you will discover that a great deal of that success is due to the fact that they were willing to be countercultural. Are you willing?

Purpose and Conflict

Purpose is at the heart of a countercultural family. The countercultural family clearly establishes what they are about, and it is a common unchanging purpose. In conversations they talk about becoming the-best-version-of-themselves. They celebrate this as their great common unchanging purpose, and this purpose brings stability and direction. It never changes. It is like the North Star that never moves and therefore is always true to those who seek guidance.

The greatest advantage this common unchanging purpose gives families is in the area of conflict.

Conflict is inevitable in relationships. This is especially true in families because you have different people, sometimes many people, of different ages and interests, all of whom are at different places in their journeys—all of which breeds inevitable conflict. Not because people are bad or wrong, but rather because people are people—unique and wonderfully different.

Often, in families, we spend a lot of time trying to avoid or calm conflict. This is usually a role parents play, but sometimes there is a child or a grandparent who takes on the role of "peacemaker" within the family. Often our approach is peace at any price, which of course is no peace at all.

We are uncomfortable with conflict because in many cases we have been raised to believe that conflict is bad. When conflict is disrespectful and rude, arrogant and selfish, it is bad. But why? Not because it is conflict. It is bad because it is unhealthy, and it is unhealthy because it doesn't help people grow and become better-versions-of-themselves. But conflict in and of itself is not bad. In fact, it can be a very powerful dynamic in relationships and families.

What we need is healthy conflict, and only one thing makes healthy conflict possible: common, unchanging purpose.

As a nation, America has this common, unchanging purpose. We find it set out in the Constitution. Certainly there have been amendments, but twenty-six Amendments in two hundred years is a phenomenal testament to the unchanging core that the framers of the Constitution set forth. The reason the Constitution (common, unchanging purpose) is so powerful is because it provides guidance and direction in times of uncertainty, transition, and disagreement. When America has an opportunity, we look to the Constitution to check that we are moving in the right direction. When

America has a crisis, we once again look to the Constitution for insight about how to best handle the crisis. The Constitution allows America to handle every situation in a way that is true to herself. It is a powerful tool without which many other nations have suffered unimaginable trials.

As individuals we, too, need a common, unchanging purpose. We spoke of it earlier though we did not call it such. Your unchanging purpose is to become the-best-version-of-yourself. It will not change when you get a little older. It was not different when you were a little younger. Though you may not have always been aware of it, it was there, dwelling within you, waiting to be discovered and pursued. In every moment of the day, in each decision, all you have to do is ask yourself: Is what I am about to do or say going to help me become the-best-version-of-myself? This one question can be a tremendous guide.

In relationships, we also need a common, unchanging purpose. Otherwise, relationships come unglued. You cannot have two people running in different directions and expect to hold that relationship together. You can have very different and varied interests and careers, but at the core, if the relationship is to be dynamic, successful, and lasting, it requires a common purpose. Common interests are not enough, we need a common, unchanging *purpose*. And the common, unchanging purpose of every relationship is to help each other become the-best-version-of-ourselves. This is true in every relationship whether that relationship is between husband and wife, boyfriend and girlfriend, brother and sister, parent and child, or between friends and colleagues. We are here to help one another become our best selves.

In a family, it is our role to help one another celebrate this common, unchanging purpose. It is not the parents' responsibility solely; it is everyone's responsibility. Even newborn babies play a role in helping others become the-best-version-of-themselves. They do it by causing people to slow down and marvel at life.

The common, unchanging purpose of every family, and each member of a family, is to help one another become the-best-version-of-themselves.

Once this is established, healthy conflict is possible. The reason why is because now, when you have an argument, rather than arguing against one another, you can argue for something. You can say to me, "Matthew, I think we should do this because it will help us become the-best-version-of-ourselves." And I can say, "I think it will stop us from becoming the-best-version-of-ourselves, and here's why." We are now arguing for something—our common, unchanging purpose—rather than arguing against each other. Now our argument becomes a quest for what is best for us rather than a battle of the egos.

Place this common, unchanging purpose at the center of your family. If you have teenagers you will need to get their buy-in. If they won't commit to it, you will not be able to create the dynamic. Because unless people commit to it, when there is a disagreement you will each be arguing with different purposes in mind. Winston Churchill and Adolf Hitler were not going to sit down and work out their differences, because they had opposing purposes.

If your children are very young you are at a great advantage, because you can introduce this concept to your family's daily culture and they will pick it up and celebrate it. Not because you are brainwashing them with it, but because they have not been affected by the nonvision and purposelessness of the culture. This dream to become the-best-version-of-ourselves is within us all. As parents and siblings we simply have to encourage it in one another and draw it out.

This is easily understood with a simple example. Say a child, perhaps four or five years old, comes to you and asks, "Can I do . . . this?" or "Can I have . . . that?" Ask that child in response, "Is that going to help you become the-best-version-of-yourself?" If the child is old enough to understand the concept, he knows instantly. The age may vary, but once a child understands the concept, he or she will know what things do and what things don't help them toward that purpose. The concept does not need explanation because we all hold within us a vision of the-best-version-of-ourselves.

As they get older, this common, unchanging purpose provides the reason. When they ask why they can't do certain things or why they shouldn't act in certain ways or go to certain places, the answer is not "Because I said so!" But rather "Because it won't help you become a-better-version-of-yourself!"

Certainly, as parents, it is important to articulate this concept. At different times you need to explain that you see your role as helping them become the-best-version-of-themselves. Explain that you don't see parenting as a popularity contest, but as a role you take seriously. When you write them birthday cards reaffirm this message. In camp letters, graduation letters, relate all things to this great purpose. It is not enough for people to hear something once or twice. The messaging of the culture is constant and repetitive almost to the point of tedium, but it works. If your messaging is going to compete it needs to be concise and constant. Is that going to help you become the-best-version-of-yourself? Are you helping your friends become the-best-version-of-themselves? Are they helping you? What can I do as a parent to help you become the-best-version-of-yourself? Let's go work out together, it will help us become better-versions-of-ourselves. Let's not go to the drive-through, we'll go home and I'll make some turkey sandwiches, it'll help us become the-best-version-of-ourselves.

Will you get all sorts of comments from them about how they have heard it before and they are sick of hearing it? You bet you will. But that is affirmation that they are hearing the message. The repetition will put the concept in their mind, and before too long, at each juncture in their day, they will start asking themselves the question.

Could you have a better dream for a child than to want him or her to become the-best-version-of-himself or -herself? It's the ultimate dream. If they are only going to hear one message from you in their entire life, make it this one. It will lead them to everything that is good, true, and noble.

And if you really want this message to sink deep into the hearts and minds of your children, make yourself vulnerable and allow them to hold you accountable. When did you last ask your children for advice or feedback? Ask them how they think you could become a-better-version-of-yourself?

I have heard hundreds of stories from parents who have used this message with their children and have had their children turn it back on them. There is no point telling them they shouldn't use foul language if you use it. If you encourage your children to eat foods that are healthy and not to watch too much television, but plant yourself in your La-Z-Boy recliner on a Sunday afternoon with a six-pack of beer and a 300-ounce bag of potato chips to watch football . . . you can expect some feedback about that. Your children will hold you rigorously accountable. Don't be surprised by it. Encourage it. Embrace it. Allow them to hold you accountable. Give them permission to hold you accountable. Thank them for helping you. However you respond to their challenge is how they will respond when you challenge them.

Everyone in a family plays a role in each member becoming his or her best self. Remind children that they have a responsibility to help you. It is not a one-way street. We are all in this together.

Conflict is inevitable. The best relationships and families are not those without conflict, but those where the conflict is dynamic, lively, healthy, and respectful. Clearly establishing a sense of purpose within the family makes that healthy conflict possible. And once we have established that we are here to help one another become the-best-version-of-ourselves, every conflict becomes an opportunity to affirm that purpose.

2

My Family

n my mind, I had a wonderful childhood . . . partly because I did and partly because I tend to forget the bad things. I grew up in Sydney, Australia, with my parents—Bernard and Jenny—and my seven brothers—Mark, Simon, Andrew, Brett, Nathan, Bernard, and Hamish. I was born in 1973, two years after Andrew and one year before Brett, and for as long as I can remember the Kelly family has lived at 104 Beresford Road.

My Parents

People often ask me about my parents. I never quite know what to say. My father was born in London. He was an only child and came to live in Australia in his mid-twenties. He used to tell us stories about the poverty he experienced as a child. When we were very young my brothers and I would often laugh and say "Sure Dad" in disbelief, as if he were telling old wives' tales again. My father was a perfect gentleman and the only man I have known whose word was better than a signed contract. My mother was born in Australia, the youngest of four. Like most women she has an amazing inner strength that lies undetected until it is needed. She handled the ups and downs of daily life amid nine males with a wonderful sense of humor. Mum says she always wanted boys. "Boys are easier," I can hear her saying. Secretly, I think my father would have loved a daughter, and when my mother was pregnant with Hamish, my youngest brother, I remember wondering how our lives would change if my mother had a girl.

As a child, I never wondered if my parents would get a divorce. The thought never crossed my mind. This may sound random or even silly, but the love between my parents was the rock upon which my character developed. Every day I was reminded of my parents' love for each other. My father never left the house of a morning without kissing my mother good-bye. I would often walk in on them kissing and hugging in the kitchen, where my mother was preparing dinner, just after my father had come home from work.

There was never any question in my mind, I knew they loved each other. Maybe it was the way they held hands when we were out, or the sixty-second phone calls (before cell phones) throughout the day for no reason other than to see how each other's day was going. Perhaps it was the way they would talk about each other with the greatest respect and admiration, or the way they took personally any disrespect shown toward the other. Maybe it was the way they were always complimenting each other for the smallest things, or the way they thanked each other, or the way they remembered things—birthdays, anniversaries, small requests. My parents noticed things about each other—haircuts, new shoes, a striking piece of clothing. They celebrated their love, and my brothers and I knew we were each a celebration of that love.

When we were very young my mother would tuck us into bed at night, read us a story, and kiss us all good night. I remember our bunk beds, two sets to a room. My mother would sit between the rooms and read our bedtime story. When this evening ritual was finished, she would slowly make her way downstairs. At the top of the stairs she would call out "I love you boys," and we would reply in unison, "I love you, too, Mum." Then, as she crept down the stairs, someone would call out again, "I love you, Mum," and she would reply, "I love you, Nathan." Then another, "I love you, Mum," and she would reply, "I love you, too, Andrew." One after the other, until everyone had taken their turn.

I think my parents did an extraordinary job raising eight boys. They were not perfect and neither are their children. They would both readily admit to making many mistakes, but they did the best they knew how. From time to time, my brothers and I have disappointed our parents, our family, and ourselves. But those moments are not a reflection of our mother and father; they are simply a necessary part of our journey toward self-discovery.

As I reminisce about my childhood, my mind is flooded with many wonderful memories. From the perspective of this modern culture I sometimes look back and wonder if I grew up in another world. In recent years I have spent endless hours wondering what my parents' parenting secrets were. I have come to some very simple conclusions. First, they always encouraged each of us to be ourselves. They did this by fostering our varied and individual interests. In a practical sense they achieved this by spending time with each of us one-on-one. When I first became interested in art, my mother started taking me to the art gallery. This was one of the ways she and I spent time alone. It was probably only once a year that we visited the art gallery, but having her undivided attention gave us an opportunity to talk about things that we would not necessarily discuss with my brothers around. We would walk the exhibit and then sit in the coffee shop and just talk. When I started playing competition golf, my father would drive me to the matches and walk the course with me. In the same way, depending on their interests, they spent time with each of my brothers. I believe it is this one-on-one time with our parents that prevented my brothers and me from feeling like just part of the crowd, and perhaps more important, from becoming just one of the crowd.

My second discovery is that my parents were excellent at giving compliments. Not the false and shallow kind, but the real and honest compliments that noted improvement or achievement. The constant stream of compliments that flowed toward each of us gave us courage and confidence to press on. My adult life has taught me that nothing helps a person bloom like an honest compliment.

And finally, when examining my parents' parenting, there is one thing that I marvel at. I cannot recall one important event in my childhood when one of my parents was not there. My parents didn't do a lot of socializing, and they don't have much in the way of hobbies, but they indulged each of us boys with plenty of carefree timelessness. They defined quality time with their children as "lots of time."

I doubt anybody will ever write a book about my parents, but they have lived worthily. My brothers and I, and our children, and our children's children will carry their torch to other places and other times. The goodness of my parent's lives will never die.

From my father I have inherited his clear thinking, reflective nature, and a small portion of his integrity, which I pray will increase over time. From my mother I have inherited a passion for the simple things in life and a very small portion of her inner strength, which I also pray will increase.

With each passing day I grow increasingly aware of my parents' shortcomings and failures. But despite all these, as time passes, I also grow increasingly appreciative of all the sacrifices they have made to love me.

I have been loved . . . and that is no small thing.

The Kelly Boys

For as long as I can remember, people have called my brothers and me "the Kelly boys." From time to time, someone will come up to one of us at a party and ask, "Are you Simon Kelly's brother?" or, after introducing myself, someone will ask, "Are you one of the Kelly boys from Strathfield?" I would not say that we all look alike, but there is a striking similarity among us. Although people have been trying to lump us all together our whole lives, my brothers are a remarkable collection of individuals. Each one is as unique and different as the next. People sometimes ask me, "Are all your brothers like you?" They are not.

My parents raised each of us to believe that we are here for some purpose. They encouraged brotherly love and unity among us, but at the same time they stressed how important it is for each of us to develop a strong sense of self and to walk our own individual paths.

Mark, my eldest brother, inherited a larger portion of my father's quiet wisdom and integrity than I did, and in the years leading up to his death he became a close confidant and counselor to me. But for most of my childhood, Mark lived in Melbourne with his wife, Christine, and their daughters, Emma and Zoe. Melbourne is Australia's second largest city and is about one thousand kilometers south of Sydney. So for many years I only saw Mark once a year. But their move to Sydney in 1998 brought a new and refreshing dynamic to family gatherings at 104 Beresford Road. Mark taught me things about relationships and raising a family that I was too young to learn from my parents as they were learning these things, and I feel privileged to have had him as a brother and friend. In 2004, he was tragically killed in a car accident. It still has not settled in. I still go to pick up the phone to call him and tell him about something some days . . . he is missed.

My brother Simon is like no other person I have ever met, or expect to meet. He is loud and boisterous. He is perpetual motion. He is the life of the party. Everybody knows Simon Kelly. He is twelve years older than I am and in my early teen years played a very important role in my development. Simon always used to take my brothers and me places. Not all together, but one at a time. He would take us to the movies, to football games, to theme parks, or just out for lunch. He would talk with us in a way that my parents couldn't. Not because there was anything wrong with the way our parents would talk with us, but because there are some things that are better discussed with a big brother. Simon is one of the most generous people I know. Most people's greatest strength is also their greatest weakness, and I sometimes believe this to be true of my brother Simon. He has a good heart and has always been an inspiration to me. In my short lifetime I have learned that there are few things as enjoyable as a good laugh. My brother Simon is the funniest person I know. He has a very broad base of knowledge . . . sports, the arts, politics, international news, popular culture . . . and is quick, witty, and absolutely hilarious. There is rarely a time when I sit down with Simon and don't get up with cramps in my cheeks from laughing so much.

Andrew is the brother directly older than me. He has the most amazing ability to endure pain. I have never seen anything like it in a man. It is of course common in women, but much rarer in men. He inherited a much greater portion of my mother's quiet inner strength. This quality naturally led Andrew to gravitate toward endurance sports—long-distance swimming and running, but predominantly cycling. For almost ten years Andrew rode a hundred kilometers a day on his bike. I have always admired his ability to push himself further than others were willing or able to, and for years have been striving to emulate it in myself.

It is here that I find my place in the lineup, after Andrew and before Brett.

Brett is a genius. He has one of the most extraordinary intellects I have ever experienced firsthand. I have observed this quality in him for many years now. At first I suspected, as we often do with extraordinary talent, that it was just a natural gift. But in time I have come to discover that the basis of this gift, and everything else he excels at, is a very firm foundation of discipline. He has an incredibly strong mind. As with Simon, his strength can also be his weakness. Everyone who knows Brett knows that he can be very willful at times. My brother Brett has sought out and achieved excellence at everything he has ever turned his hand to.

Nathan is fifth from the top and third from the bottom. As a child, Nathan was often rebellious. Some people thought him a rough-and-tough troublemaker. But deep down Nathan is a very, very sensitive person. He is a lover of poetry and an admirer of beauty wherever it is to be found. Nathan is an artist in the universal sense of the word. Art is not something he does, but rather the way he approaches life. He hates the lie of modern culture. He despises hypocrisy, and he has a bit of a temper. Nothing will ignite that temper like injustice or hypocrisy. Nathan suffers under the weight of the integrity that we associate with an artist, which lifts a man above the level of the world without delivering him from it. What I love most about Nathan is his personality. When he wants to, Nathan has the most mesmerizing, charming, and enchanting personality I have ever known. I think it's because he is so accepting of people, wherever they are in their lives. Nathan doesn't seek to control or change people. He just enjoys them for who they are and where they are, right now.

Bernard is the seventh son. In Irish folklore, the seventh son of the seventh son was believed to be endowed with special gifts. I think the Irishman who came up with that saying just figured that the odds of having seven sons was pretty slim, then if you add to that the fact that the seventh son also has to have seven sons, the odds are near impossible. Incidentally, what do you think the odds of having eight boys and no girls are? Anyway . . . although Bernard is not the seventh son of a seventh son, he has special gifts. He has an uncanny ability to read people. I noticed this for the first time when he was about thirteen. One of my brothers asked him, "What do you think of so-and-so?" The answer he gave was so incredibly perceptive that I was awestruck. When you first meet Bernard it is easy to underestimate him. Don't be fooled. He is all there and all together. My brother Bernard is the hardest worker I know. If I could find five people to work as hard as he does to help me with my work, I think we could probably change the world. One thing is certain, when Bernard decides he is going to do something, help him or get out of the way, he is total dedication.

Hamish is my baby brother, the youngest of the Kelly boys. In some ways I have often thought he grew up in the shadowlands. My brothers are charming, intelligent, and funny; they are champions of selfhood; and each of them in their own way is an overachiever. Some of my brothers cast some pretty big shadows, and Hamish has had to grow up amid those shadows. This has been hard for him I think. Each of us must find our own way in this life, but there are so many influences and distractions, and I sense this search for self has been made more difficult for Hamish by his brothers' successes. As I am writing these words Hamish is still young. Time is on his side. I pray that he will be patient with himself, that he will believe that his path will emerge, and that when it does, he will have the courage to follow it. Whenever I see Hamish I just want to hug him. Who he is, and the joy he has brought to our lives as a family, makes him irresistibly adorable. He, too, has enormous personality and magnetism, but sometimes he allows himself to be overcome by discouragement. I hope in time the former will triumph more and more.

These are my brothers. I could tell you tales for days about our childhood together that would make you laugh, cry, and no doubt wonder.

I have told you who my brothers are, and compared to who they are what they do is trivial information, but all the same I will satisfy your curiosity. Mark was an executive for Australia's leading supermarket chain, Simon is a financial adviser, Andrew is a banker turned entrepreneur, Brett is an accountant, Nathan is a professional photographer and schoolteacher, Bernard is a consultant to McDonald's, and Hamish is a security guard. I am an author, a speaker, and a business consultant, but to them I am just their brother Matthew. At times that is the most liberating of all realities. To be loved and enjoyed simply for who you are independent of what you do.

Dinner at Six

Every evening while I was growing up, my family came together for dinner. The television was turned off, radios were turned off, homework was put aside, and everyone in the house took their place around the dinner table. I never had to ask my mother what time dinner would be. Dinner was at six o'clock. As I look back upon my childhood, I discover that there were a great many rituals that took place with unerring consistency.

My parents created a lifestyle, a family culture, that fostered a deep sense of stability in my brothers and me. In times of peace a nation turns its attention away from defending itself, away from merely surviving, and begins to focus on growing, developing, and thriving. The same is true in children. When children sense stability, a hundred fears subside and they almost naturally begin to bloom. There was routine to the days of my childhood, and that routine created a certain sense of stability. As a culture we have rejected the wisdom of routine, but it is and always will be the fertile soil in which true character is developed.

Dinner always began with grace, each night the same prayer, led by one of the boys but sung in unison by us all: "The Lord is good to me and so I thank the Lord, for giving me the things I need, the sun and the rain, and the apple seed. The Lord is good to me. Amen."

As I have grown older I have come to appreciate my mother's giftedness more and more. Every night she presented something wonderful for dinner. Sometimes it was your favorite, and sometimes it wasn't. My dear mother would often try to introduce us to more refined dishes. She would spend all day preparing a special meal, then at dinnertime, we would sit down and inevitably someone would say out of disappointment or disgust, "What is this?" How my mother's heart must have suffered at times living in a house full of males. But every night dinner was good and hot, and no matter how much food mum prepared, there was never any left.

Once we had settled into the meal and everybody had salt, pepper, bread, butter, and tomato sauce—which is what we call ketchup in Australia—my father would then move around the table and ask each of his sons, "How was your day?" "Fine" or "Good" were not acceptable answers. Each of us knew and understood that we were expected to share a piece of our day. Perhaps something we learned in school, perhaps some news about a friend or teacher, perhaps something that happened at training. Dad would listen to each of us and ask questions to draw us out just that little bit more. This way everyone had an opportunity to speak at every meal. When each of the boys had dialogued with Dad, my father would then turn to my mother and ask her about her day, and then vice versa. It sounds very civilized, but my brothers are not exactly the quiet, shy type. They always seemed to have some comment. Depending on who said what, the scene would often descend into something vaguely resembling what you sometimes see in Congress or Parliament when a controversial issue is being discussed. Cheering and jeering, snide comments and bickering, words muttered under the breath, and on occasion full-on confrontation.

In my travels, many people have asked about how I overcame the nervousness and other difficulties usually associated with public speaking. I tell them that speaking to large groups of people, even ten thousand at a time, is nothing compared to trying to voice an opinion at the dinner table in the Kelly household. They laugh. They think I'm joking . . . I'm not.

The kindness and gentleness of my parents, their impeccable manners and sense of place, were often opposed by the harshness of my brothers and me passing through the various stages of growing up. As brothers, we were also brutally cruel to one another at times. But all in all, the dinner table was a wonderful place, a wonderful experience, and an exciting event. You never knew what was going to happen.

As a very young child, I vaguely remember my brothers Mark and Simon fighting over who was going to do the dishes. By the time I was old enough to be involved with this dimension of family life, we had a dishwasher. So we fought over who was going to load the dishwasher. This was one of those ritual arguments that never should have taken place. Each person packed the dishwasher one night a week, and the system flowed from the eldest brother to the youngest able to do the task. I do remember Nathan once complaining because it was his turn and he didn't feel like it. So he entered into a philosophical discussion, which quickly turned south and became a full-fledged argument with my mother, who was more than capable of holding her own. The main theme of his argument was that "it wasn't fair" because Hamish never packed the dishwasher. The weakness in his argument was that at the time Hamish was three years old.

As I grew older, I learned a great deal just by coming to dinner each night. Everything was discussed—sports, art, politics, world news, literature, music, and of course business. By the time I got to business school at the age of eighteen, I am certain I had picked up enough at the dinner table to see me through my degree. The dinner table at Beresford Road was my first business school. Dinner was a cultural experience, but above everything else, it was a time of family. Dinner at six was a constant in the changing seasons of our

individual lives, and a touchstone in the ever-changing challenges of our life as a family. We took it for granted, but if I
ever have children, I hope I can give them "dinner at six."

This is how we talk about our families. We put our best foot
forward. It's like the Christmas cards and letters that only
show us in our best light. We report the highlights of the year,
and bury anything that might be shameful and embarrassing.
I have a wonderful family, but just so you are not under any
illusions, my family can put the "fun" in dysfunctional with
the best of them at times. There is dysfunction in all families.
Mine is no different, and I would not want you to think otherwise.

3

Parenting in the Twenty-first Century

On the news today was the story of a young man, just graduated from college, who, like so many graduates, had gone straight from graduation to Daytona Beach for a week of partying. Last night he came back to his hotel room completely drunk, went into the bathroom, fell over, and broke his neck. Three days after graduation, with all the talk of having his whole life ahead of him, and—he's dead.

What are his parents feeling? Just days ago they were full of happiness for their son and themselves. For twenty-two years they had supported him, nurtured him, encouraged him, and loved him—and now he is gone. What is that pain like? And what questions do they ask themselves when they are lying awake at night? Do they feel responsible? Do they wish they had done something differently along the way? What happened was a horrific accident. It could happen to anyone—drunk *or* sober.

At graduation, they probably thought their responsibilities as parents were just about over and were patting each other on the back. But now, filled with an indescribable pain and a grief that won't go away, do they second-guess their parenting? I would think that would be natural. The farthest thing from the minds of parents is that their child will die before them, but every day parents mourn the death of their children. Parents who have lost a child will tell you that it is a mourning that never ends.

In our lives, we often wait too long to reflect and celebrate, or simply reflect on things too seldom. Parenting is not something we should reflect upon and celebrate only at graduations and weddings. It is something we should reflect upon and celebrate often, perhaps every day. Parenting is not about one great success—graduation, marriage, a successful career, wealth, fame, status. No, parenting is about everyday success. At the end of each day we should be able to look at the parenting stoplight and think: Green, yellow, or red? This simple self-assessment allows us to gauge how we are doing as parents. If you assess yourself as a red today, you know why, and chances are you know what to do about it. If you assess yourself as yellow today, the same is probably true. If you assess yourself as green, you know tomorrow is a new day and it is likely going to take all the patience and self-possession you can muster to do it again. Success as a parent doesn't come in one fell swoop. Parenting success is one day at a time.

What Makes a Successful Parent?

I propose this question not to further our modern-day obsession with success, but in the hope that the question itself might help us to better understand parenting and success. When it comes to parenting, we are usually subjective in the attitudes we take. There are those who think they are not good parents, most of whom really are wonderful parents.

There are some who think they are great parents, and often turn out to be inattentive and self-absorbed. Then there are others who have a healthy sense that they are not perfect, but they are genuinely making their best effort on a daily basis. The reality is, as human beings, we often find it very difficult to see ourselves as we really are, and this extends to our parenting.

Small talk at work and church and in the mall consists of the question "How are the kids?" More often than not, the answer is a rosy litany of achievements and adventures. Rarely, if ever, is the answer, "Michael's caught up in drugs, Susan is sleeping with every second guy she meets, and Jason failed every course in the ninth grade!" This is fine for the small talk, but when we lay our heads on our pillows at night, how do we measure how our children really are, and how do we grade ourselves as parents?

In assessing our success as parents we tend to apply very subjective parameters. We compare our children with their peers, with their siblings, with their neighbors—older and younger, and we tend to make excuses for any glaring defects or monumental mistakes. "He was just doing what young men do." "That is part of discovering who she is." "The world is different today from when we were young."

For most parents, the perception that they have done well, or are doing well as parents, is nothing more than that: a perception. They may have been the best parents in the world, they may have been massively negligent and unaware of it, and yet, their perception is that they have done well. But compared to what? How do we measure? What yardstick should we use? How could we know for sure? In this chapter

I want to explore this issue in some detail. When it comes to parenting, what does it mean to do well? What does success look like?

My first observation is that when we judge someone's success as a parent, our own or somebody else's, we immediately look to the children. We then tend to take a snapshot of where that child is in his or her journey, assess successes and failures, and judge based upon a personal and subjective set of criteria. We completely overlook the fact that this child, this person, is a work in progress. We usually exaggerate the negative or the positive depending on our prejudices. All of which is extremely subjective.

But is there some yardstick by which we could objectively look at ourselves and others and assess progress? There is: virtue.

Keep in mind that life is about relationships. Relationships between husbands and wives, parents and children, friends and colleagues, business associates, and nations. All are relationships. And at the heart of a relationship we find one immutable and universal truth: two virtuous people will always have a better relationship than two who lack virtue. Consider it practically. Two patient people will always have a better relationship than two impatient people. Kind and generous people will always have a better relationship than selfish people. Two thoughtful people will always have a better relationship than two thoughtless people. At the core of dynamic and lasting relationships is the bedrock of virtue. Certainly, there are many cases where we see cowardice (and other vices) dressed up and pretending to be any number of virtues. I am not talking about this. I am talking about genuine virtue.

If life is about relationships, and parenting is about preparing children for life. In its very best form, successful parenting is a school of virtue. It is the quality we should be looking for in our children. Are they kind, patient, honest, just, temperate, courageous, loving, humble, thoughtful, gentle, compassionate, persevering?

But maybe we obsess too much over the qualities we are looking for in our children. Let's face it, you have no direct control over what your children do. Any parent who has had a particularly obstinate or disobedient child will tell you that. We may think we have control over what our children do, but in reality it would only take the turning of their will to prove that we don't.

On the other hand, we have almost complete control over what we do ourselves. This is where we should place our focus. What we do has more influence upon our children than anything we say or any use of parental authority. And virtue is the pinnacle of human action and achievement. Successful parenting can be measured one day at a time by asking, "Today, was I kind, patient, honest, just, temperate, courageous, loving, humble, thoughtful, gentle, compassionate, persevering?"

If we are striving to live and model virtue for our children, we need to foster a certain detachment from the outcome. Having attended a school of virtue, they must then go out into the world and make their own choices and decisions. In every moment they will be required, just as you and I are, to choose between virtue and vice, to choose between the-best-version-of-themselves and some second-rate version.

This detachment from the outcome is very difficult to achieve. Often, just when you think you have developed it, something happens and you realize you haven't. When I am training Dream Managers, I have to make this very same point over and over, and over again. A Dream Manager is a life coach who helps people identify their dreams, prepare a strategic plan for the achievement of those dreams, and holds them accountable to the steps they identify as necessary to achieve their dreams. It is not the Dream Manager's job to accomplish the dreams for their clients, but simply to help them create a strategy, encourage them along the way, and hold them accountable to what they said they would do. The best Dream Managers recognize that their job is to present the material to the best of their ability and to be a source of encouragement and support, but that they are not responsible for the outcome.

I meet wonderful people all the time whose children have made horrible decisions. Are they bad parents? For the most part, I don't think so. There comes a point in our lives when we must choose what life we want to live and who we are going to become. This is a child's choice, not a parent's. All we can do as parents is point our children along the path we think is best.

But there are so many paths. How do you know which path to point your child along? One of the most successful books of the twentieth century was Stephen Covey's *The 7 Habits of Highly Effective People.* If you ask people, "How do you know it was a successful book?" most will say it's because it sold millions of copies. But they would have over-looked the real success. It was one of the most successful books of its era because it challenged and changed the way people look at themselves, the world, and their relationships; and at the same time gave them a model against which to hold themselves accountable in the moments of their lives. It changed the way people behaved. Habit #2 is of particular relevance to us here: "Begin with the end in mind."

It's important to know from the outset what "good" looks like. If we don't know where we are going, then no amount of trying will get us there. It is never too early for parents to consider what outcome they are working toward. So let me ask you two questions. The first is this: When your children are grown and out living their own lives in the world, what *one word* would you like them to use to describe you? The second is: What *one word* would you like to perfectly de-scribe your child at that time?

Let us consider the second question first. It seems children and parents spend a lot of time trying to fit in and be per-ceived as normal. Is that your word? Is *normal* the one word you would use to describe your child when he or she is out living his or her life? If it isn't, why do we do so much parent-ing toward normal? Besides, have you taken a look at what normal looks like lately? If by normal we mean in tune with what most other people their age are doing, is that really what you want?

What one word would you pick for your child? Loving, confident, contributing, successful, wealthy, famous, kind, prayerful, virtuous, admired . . . or perhaps you would like to be able to say, "My child is a person of 'character.'"

Some parents want their children to be famous and they very much parent toward that word, though they would rarely admit it and always insist it is for the good of the child. Many parents would say that the one word they chose is character, but often a closer examination reveals that their day-to-day parenting is not toward that word. When asked what they want for their children, most parents say to be happy. But it is a difficult word to parent toward. As a result, the great majority of parenting is toward success, mostly because we assume that if our children are successful they will be happy, or that if they are successful they will be able to work the rest out on their own. In reality, those who were happy before they were successful tend to remain happy, and success is often an impediment (not a help) to working out who we are and what we are here for.

So, what word are you parenting toward?

The idea of parenting toward an outcome that is summarized by one word is not simply for a theoretical discussion. Each day, as a parent, you have to make dozens of decisions. The one word you choose will help you to make those decisions. In the heat of the moment you often don't have time to fully consider things. You need to be prepared for that. That's why we are doing the reflecting now, because when the moment arrives you won't necessarily have time to do the reflecting. Many situations require immediate answers. You often don't have the luxury of saying, "Let me think about it." But if you know your one word is character, that word becomes a filter that helps you to make decisions.

This brings us full circle. We have discussed what one

word you would like to use to describe your child, but what word did you choose for them to use to describe you? Is it the same one in both cases? If not, why? Either way, the one word that you would like your children to use to describe you also becomes a filter, not so much for your parenting decisions as for your personal actions. If your word is virtuous and you sense yourself becoming very impatient in a situation, you will check yourself. In this way your word becomes a guide in the moments of the day.

Then again, maybe one word is not enough. Perhaps you need a phrase, or a couple of words. For myself, I use a phrase as my filter in making decisions in every area of my life: the-best-version-of-myself. Is what I am about to eat going to help me become the-best-version-of-myself? Are my friends helping me to become the-best-version-of-myself? Is this movie . . . book . . . music . . . going to help me to become the-best-version-of-myself?

Perhaps you want to start parenting toward this. The point of this exercise is to become conscious of what we are parenting toward, because unless we know where we are going, we will never get there. If we do not know what we are trying to achieve, we will never accomplish it.

Successful parenting in the twenty-first century requires determined effort, strength of will, and clarity of purpose. In a word, character. And virtues are the building blocks of character. You cannot move a brick wall with a squirt gun. The strength of the culture that our children find themselves immersed in every day is monumental. If we want them to be able to defend and celebrate the-best-version-of-themselves, we need to do everything within our power to equip them with virtue and character, and the best way to do that is to model these things ourselves.

Are You a Leader?

When was the last time you read a book about leadership? When was the last time you thought about yourself as a leader? As a parent, you are a leader, and leadership is not a passive role. Leadership must be proactive or not at all. Young people need leadership, and in the absence of genuine leadership in their lives they will listen to anyone who steps up to the microphone. So let's take a few minutes to explore nine qualities that great leaders work hard to develop.

1. GREAT LEADERS ARE VISIONARIES

Marcus Aurelius had a vision for Rome. The Founding Fathers had a vision for America. Leaders are visionaries. Your vision does not need to be complex or revolutionary or radically original. The best insights are usually the simplest ones. What is your vision for your family? Do you know? If you don't then it is impossible to communicate to your children what your vision is.

If you accept the idea that we are each here on earth to become the-best-version-of-ourselves, and to help each other in that quest, then you have your vision. The next step is to communicate and overcommunicate the vision. As a parent, you are probably more aware than most leaders that it is not enough to say something once. Whatever message you want to convey to the people you are leading—your children—you need to continually communicate that message and reinforce it with your example.

A large part of parenting is developing your skills as a leader, and great leaders have a vision. So, you need a vision—for yourself, for your children, for your family.

2. GREAT LEADERS ARE DECISIVE

Once you have established your vision, it becomes a powerful organizing tool. The life of a parent is crammed with a thousand activities and decisions every week. Your vision helps you to prioritize what activities are most important. Without a vision, the things that matter most tend to suffer at the hands of those things that matter least. It is not enough just to be doing things. Leaders don't just lead people to do things; they lead them to do the right things. Vision gives birth to priorities.

The other great practical gift that vision gives us is decisiveness. Every day you make decisions as a parent, but how do you make them? Does it depend on your mood? If you're tired, do your children know that they can get away with certain things and wait until you are tired to raise certain topics?

Once you set your vision, it becomes the common, unchanging factor in your decision-making. By asking one or two simple questions, you can now confidently arrive at decisions that in the past you may have agonized over for days. Is this going to help my child to become a-better-version-of-him or -herself? Is this going to help my family become a-better-version-of-itself?

Decisiveness is one of the hallmarks of great leaders.

3. GREAT LEADERS LEAD BY EXAMPLE

There is nothing more powerful than authenticity. It has always been true, but particularly in our day and age where nothing and no one seem to be what they appear to be. Young people especially have incredible instincts when it comes to sniffing out the authentic. Great leaders don't lead with words, they lead with action.

Example trumps all else when it comes to leadership. Being willing to get in and do what you are asking others to do will always be respected by those you are trying to lead. There is no point telling a child not to smoke if you are a smoker. It doesn't matter how good your motives are. It doesn't matter how grand your vision is or how good you are at communicating that vision. How does the old saying go? What you do screams so loudly that I cannot hear what you say.

If you want to convince your child to eat nourishing foods and exercise regularly, it is not enough simply to tell them to do it. It is not enough to tell them that it will help them become the-best-version-of-themselves. It is a grand vision, but visions are empty without example. It is not enough to explain that they will be healthier and happier. What is needed is a leader who eats foods that are nourishing, exercises regularly, and is clearly healthier and happier because of it.

Children will gladly follow where you are willing to lead

them yourself. They become skeptical and questioning of those who simply stand still and point them down a path.

4. GREAT LEADERS ARE TRUSTWORTHY

Having the right vision endears people to trust you. Demonstrating good decision-making skills endears people to trust you. Leading by example endears people to trust you. But can you be trusted? Every relationship revolves around this question.

When you take your thirteen-year-old to an event and there is a special price for children twelve and under, what do you do? Many people tell their children to say they are twelve. My older brothers used to tell me to do that. You may save a few dollars, but what is the real cost? You are teaching your children that it is okay to lie sometimes. You are teaching them how to lie and desensitizing them to the division we create within ourselves by lying. You are communicating to them that you are a liar and are essentially teaching them to lie to you in the not too distant future.

Your word is your oath. If what you say cannot be trusted, you completely undermine your ability to lead. It is hard enough to lead people who trust you, never mind trying to lead those who are always second-guessing you because they are trying to work out if you are being honest.

Great leaders understand the power of truth. They celebrate the truth, even when that involves tough decisions and the loss of popularity. In the long term, nothing serves a leader like the truth. To a certain extent, you can lose trust through lack of vision, by being indecisive, or by being unwilling to lead by example. But the leader whose word can-not be trusted quickly becomes disabled.

5. GREAT LEADERS ARE STORYTELLERS

Some people think that to be a great leader you need to be charismatic, but it is not true. There are plenty of examples in business and politics of not so charismatic leaders who were phenomenally effective. But to be a great leader you do have to be a good storyteller.

People need to be inspired. We don't do anything until we are inspired. Education is not enough, we need inspiration. A large part of my work involves inspiring people and organizations to give their lives to something worthy and to become all that they are capable of being. Speaking and writing, I am constantly hoping to inspire people to build a future better than their past for themselves, their families, their nations, and for the world. And yet, even though this is what I do for millions of people in dozens of countries around the world, I still need to be inspired every day. For this reason, I constantly listen to audio programs, read great books and articles, and try to surround myself with interesting and inspiring people. We all need to be inspired.

The most powerful people in history are storytellers. The reason is because we become the stories we listen to. It doesn't matter if the storyteller is Adolf Hitler in Nazi Germany or Abraham Lincoln during the American Civil War, we become the stories we listen to. Great leaders understand the power of stories, and they communicate inspiring stories to the people they lead.

What stories are your children listening to? They hear stories through music, movies, books, video games, magazines, the Internet, television—and they are becoming the stories they listen to. It's a little frightening when you consider the collage of stories the average child is being exposed to. Perhaps we need to reconsider what stories we expose our children to?

But on another level, and in the first place, we need to consider what stories we are telling our children. I am not talking about the stories we read young children before they go to bed, though these certainly play a powerful role in their development. I am talking about the stories we tell our children in conversation and through our example.

The most powerful story you tell the world every day is the story of how you choose to live your life. This story, your story, affects the lives of everyone who crosses your path . . . and millions of people whom you will never meet or know. Our lives are not a private matter; they are a public act with global repercussions. The way you live your life will be affecting people for generations to come until the end of time. What story are you telling with your life? This story will have more impact on your children than any other single factor in their lives. Psychologists' offices are filled every day with people trying to make sense of the story their parents told them.

Beyond this very intimate story of your life, let us also consider the stories we tell each other and our children in conversation. Are we constantly talking about the latest horrific world event or do we talk about the people who we look up to and why? Are we constantly discussing fame and fortune or do we make time to speak of the ordinary people who are our heroes and mentors? Do you tell your children what you loved about your parents and grandparents? Do they know the stories of the teachers and coaches who had the most influence on your life? Do they know the story of your life? Have you told them the story of how you met their mother or father?

Stories are powerful, and great leaders continuously develop an inspiring repertoire to have on hand when the right moment arises.

6. GREAT LEADERS ARE COLLABORATORS

You can't do it all yourself. You need partners to collaborate with in your parenting quest. Your leadership will only ever be as strong and broad as your ability to collaborate.

Parenting is not a solo job, even for a single parent. Yes, in the traditional scenario, your primary partner in your role as a parent would be your husband or wife, but beyond this parenting collaboration there are many partnerships to consider. These partners may include: your parents, your brothers and sisters, neighbors, friends, teachers and coaches at school, your older children, and so on. It's important that you work out who is on your team. In your parenting quest, who are your partners and collaborators?

It is also of paramount importance to recognize that your child, too, is your collaborator in the process of parenting. This is why it is important to clearly communicate the vision to them, and to enlist their help. Appeal to them for help. Explain the great vision you are working toward with them and ask them to participate in making that vision a reality.

Collaboration suggests that we are all rowing in the same direction. So, once you have determined who your collaborators are, you need to communicate your vision to them. Tell your child's teachers and coaches: "I want to do everything I can to encourage my child to become the-best-version-of-herself. This is the language I use to communicate with her. It would be great if you could reinforce this idea with this language." What you will discover is that most people don't have a vision, and if your vision is compelling, they will gladly support you in it, and, even better, they will adopt it as their own. Before long, the teacher or coach will be encouraging all his students to become the-best-version-of-themselves.

Great leaders know they cannot do everything on their own, and they expand their influence by choosing great partners to collaborate with.

7. GREAT LEADERS ARE PERSUASIVE

When children are young, it is easy to rule over them with your power and authority as a parent. This works with reasonable success until finally the child rebels against this type of parenting. Why? Because it is tyrannical leadership, and you and I would rebel in the same way. Great leaders are much more interested in using the power of persuasion than they are in using the raw power of authority.

I am not suggesting you try to persuade a two-year-old throwing a tantrum in the middle of the supermarket that the chocolate bar she insists on having will not help her to reach her full potential as a human being. Not at all. There will be times when you will need to display your raw authority as a parent. But leaders use this raw authority sparingly, and never unnecessarily.

The art of persuasion is one of the finer abilities of a great leader. We have already laid down the main requirements for effective persuasion—vision, authentic example, truth and trust, and inspiring storytelling. Now we must bring them all together to persuade our children to act. The leader who cannot persuade her followers to act is no leader at all.

The key to persuasion is convincing the other person that what you propose is in his or her best interest. The most persuasive sales people are usually those with the best products, because they believe that what they are selling will improve the life of those who purchase it. The best public speakers are usually those who believe in what they are saying. There are some salespeople and speakers who are able to sell anything or speak about anything, but they are the exception. So, in order to persuade your children to adopt your vision and to act on that vision in the moments of the day, whether you are around or not, you must first convince them that you have their best interests at heart.

It is easy for us to be selfish. For most of us, this is our default position. Only over time and with practice do we correct this and establish a default position that leads us to think of others before ourselves. It is critically important that our children believe that we want them to become the-best-version-of-themselves simply because we love them, and not because it will make our lives easier, or because we will be able to boast about them. Nothing we say will convince them of this. We can only convince children of this by the way we act.

8. GREAT LEADERS MAKE MISTAKES AND KNOW THEY DON'T HAVE ALL THE ANSWERS

For decades, the laws of business leadership have viewed vulnerability as weakness. Today, more and more leaders in a variety of realms are realizing that this is simply a psychological case of the king has no clothes on. Vulnerability doesn't weaken us as leaders, it makes us stronger. When we reveal our struggles to others, their natural inclination is to want to help. This vulnerability is difficult, but essential, to the modern leader.

There is no point pretending to your children that you never make mistakes. Soon enough, they grow old enough to realize that you do and then you lose credibility, and a leader without credibility has no one to lead but himself.

I remember once as a child getting in trouble and my mother sending me to my room. I was to stay there until my father came home. When Dad arrived home my mother briefed him on what I had done, no doubt, and then sent him to talk to me. When he came into my room, I was lying on my bed and he sat down in my desk chair. He asked me how I was and I replied, "Fine." He asked me what was happening in my life, and I said, "Nothing." I was expecting him to get mad and be angry with me, but he wasn't. Then he told me a story about a time in his life when he had done something pretty stupid. By telling me a story about how he once messed up, he made himself vulnerable. That vulnerability created a bond, a connection, an intimacy. When he was finished with his story he said, "Now, Matthew, your mother tells me you've done a stupid thing. You're a smart kid. If you keep doing things like that, what sort of a life will it lead to? Build yourself a good life, and I'm here to help you with that."

My father never even mentioned what I had done to be sent to my room, but by revealing a little about his own mistakes and faults, he gave me permission to be human. And we need that. As strange as it may seem, we need permission to be human. Children need it more than anyone else. It would be a tragedy to create a fear of failure in a child. Three hundred as a batting average makes you among the best in baseball, and I suspect the same is true in life. Great leaders make a lot of mistakes but they admit them, learn from them, and press on.

The other quality found in leaders who are secure in who they are is that they don't pretend to have all the answers. It is a mistake to think that you always have to have the answers for your children. Mostly because it stems from a pride that is dangerous in and of itself, but also because it robs you of one of your great opportunities as a parent—the opportunity to teach your children how and where to find answers to questions.

It's okay to say "I don't know!" But let's be quick to follow it up with "But let's find out!"

As a child, I was taken to the library to investigate such questions. Today I suppose it is just as easy to jump on Google, do a quick search, and find the answer. Empowering children to find answers is one of the most practical gifts we can give them as parents, and one we only think to give them after we admit we don't have all the answers. Sure, you could go off and find the answer and bring it back to them and continue the all-knowing pretense. But you would be robbing your child of a powerful life lesson.

Great leaders are not afraid to make mistakes, and they are equally unafraid to say "I don't know!"

9. GREAT LEADERS PERSEVERE

In your battle to deliver your child to a life greater than the nonvision the culture has in store for him or her, you are going to require more than your fair share of perseverance.

Before the outbreak of World War II, and even for many months into it, many people believed that Hitler could be reasoned with if the right people could get around the table and talk to him. Winston Churchill maintained from the very beginning that this wouldn't work and that force alone would bring an end to Hitler's diabolical ideas and plans. Hitler's troops advanced into Austria, Poland, Italy, and France, and still much of the world believed that he could be reasoned with. It was Churchill who roused the forces to not only defend England but to attack the German army and liberate much of Europe. It was a tough decision and one that he had to make and remain committed to day after day during the bloody battles while he watched the sons of a whole generation slaughtered across Europe. It is this same perseverance that you will be required to display as a parent.

Sometimes it may appear that your child is the enemy, but

it is never so. The enemy is the ideas and influence of a culture that has no vision for the people. At the same time, this culture is armed with the seductive charms of a thousand ages and is bringing them all to bear on your children. It is your job to give them a vision and to persevere in that vision.

These were the words Churchill used to encouraged the students at the Harrow school in 1941, which he himself had attended as a child, "Never give in! Never. Never. Never. Never. Never."

Parenting and leadership are indispensably linked. You may never have thought of your role as a parent as a leadership role, and that's okay. But start now. Children need leadership, and if you don't play the role somebody else will . . . and there is a better than good chance that they will not have your child's best interests at heart in the way you do. Step up. Begin to think about leadership, study leadership, read books about leadership, learn what it means to be a great leader. Men and woman are not born leaders. Leaders are forged one decision at a time.

What Do Children Need?

At the heart of our lives as human beings, at the very core of our existence is need. We are not as strong as we think we are. In fact, in many ways we are fragile, weak, broken, and needy. Security and stability are only illusions that are quickly banished by illness or accident. We are bound together in the adventure we call life by need, and our true strength begins to emerge when we recognize our needs and the needs of others. Knowing what a child genuinely needs, and teaching children to recognize their real and legitimate needs is one of the more difficult and subtle arts of parenting.

We tend to throw the word *need* around fairly loosely in the modern arena. I walked into a store a few weeks ago and the salesperson asked me, "What do you need today?" His question struck me and I began to think about it. The reason it struck me was because I needed absolutely nothing. I bought myself a nice pair of jeans, but I didn't really need them. I could have gotten by without them. In fact, I could probably stop buying clothes today and not genuinely need a stitch of clothing for many years.

So when we ask this question—What do children need?—what are we really talking about?

We all have legitimate needs in four areas: physical, emotional, intellectual, and spiritual. When a baby is born, if the child is not held, caressed, touched, she will die. A newborn child has a real and legitimate need to be held—her survival depends upon it. Similarly, in this very moment you have a legitimate need for air to breathe. If that air was suddenly unavailable for just a few minutes, you would die. You also need water to drink and food to eat, otherwise your very existence will be threatened. These are the most basic of our needs, but we also have needs that are significantly more subtle in that if we do not attend to them we will not die immediately. Nonetheless the neglect of these needs can lead to physical and mental illness and great unhappiness. Most of all, when we neglect our legitimate needs we hinder our ability to genuinely thrive.

The greatest threat to the fulfillment of our children's needs, and indeed our own, is the modern culture. Our present culture proclaims with unwavering authority that happiness is linked to getting what you want. Our culture is not even the slightest bit interested in our needs. The culture is obsessed with wants. The message of the culture is, "Go out and get what you want and then you will be happy." This messaging is so powerful and seductive, and the pull of our peer group's actions so equally alluring, that it is very easy to get caught up into chasing what we want. But pause for a moment and have a look around. This has been the dominant practical philosophy of our culture for more than fifty years now, and for fifty years people have been going out and getting what they want on an ever-increasing basis. But where is all the happiness that getting what we want was suppose to deliver? As best I can tell, people seem more irritable, restless, and discontented than ever before.

Why? Because the philosophy of "you go out and get what you want and then you'll be happy" doesn't work. It's a failed experiment. We know it. We have experienced the dissatisfied emptiness it delivers, but we still carry on. We tell ourselves that we didn't want enough, that our mistake was in not wanting more. We continue to chase more and more of what we want, all the time that nagging little voice within us quietly calls to us saying "You're going about this the wrong way." But we continue to ignore it out of fear or doubt or simple fatigue, and continue to tell ourselves, "If I can just get enough of what I really want, then I will be happy." But you can't. You simply never can get enough of what you don't really need.

It's impossible—not difficult, impossible. You simply cannot get enough of what you don't really need. You can only get enough of what you genuinely and legitimately need. Contentment and happiness, balance and wisdom are not arrived at by getting what we want, but by celebrating what we authentically need.

Getting what we want only feeds the ego, it does not fulfill any real need. And the ego is a monster whose appetite grows greater and greater each time we feed it. The ego is always hungry and never satisfied.

The great challenge, therefore, is to switch our focus from what we want to what we need. As we raise our children, it should help them to focus on need as they develop their decision-making skills and strengths.

So, what are our children's legitimate needs?

Physically, they need air to breathe, water to drink, food to eat, and shelter over their heads. They need to be held and hugged, and they need regular physical exercise.

Emotionally, they need to be hugged and held. Yes, it is as much an emotional need as it is a physical need. Children need to be listened to. They need to be loved, but they also desperately need opportunities to love. They need time, the time of parents, coaches, mentors, and teachers. They need to feel like someone understands them, or at least is trying to understand them. They need to know that they are not alone.

Intellectually, they need to constantly have their horizons expanded by learning new things. They need to have their curiosity encouraged. Children need to have their love of learning celebrated.

Spiritually, they need to learn to be comfortable in their

· own company. They need small doses of silence and solitude mixed in with the frenetic activity of their lives to process what they are experiencing and what it means to who they are called to be.

This is by no means a comprehensive list of the legitimate needs of a child, but I hope it gives you a sense of the breadth and depth of a child's needs.

Knowing what a child needs is one thing, giving them what they need is somthing entirely different. Sometimes it is simply impossible to give them what they need because of the daily pressures of life. Sometimes we struggle to give children what they need because of our own selfishness and inner struggles. Sometimes we are distracted and simply do not recognize their needs. And as they grow older, having their needs fulfilled becomes as much their choice as it is ours.

When you leave the hospital with a newborn child, they don't give you an instruction manual; there is no check-list when it comes to parenting. I cannot give you a list of things and say, "If you do all these things you will be a great parent and raise amazing children." There are too many variables outside of your control. With every passing year, your control and influence diminishes. Many psychologists believe that by the age of twelve, children have developed their value system. They may stray from it in the years of adolescence and young adulthood, but by twelve they have established their true north. This suggests that the years up until the age of twelve are most critical. So, having said that, there are no comprehensive guaranteed checklists. I would like to give you a short list all the same. Just five things to run through mentally from time to time and give yourself a score. The order I present them in is for ease of explanation and not priority.

1. *Your child needs you to be a parent, not a friend.* I hope you will have an amazing friendship that lasts a lifetime and grows deeper and richer with every passing year, but when it comes down to it, they need a parent much more than they need a friend. They will be able to make plenty of friends in this world, but not parents. You're it. Don't overlook your mission in all of this.

Today, many parents want to be friends with their children. The reasons why are many and varied, from looking to their children to fulfill their unmet needs, to lacking the discipline and fortitude to give a child the discipline he or she needs. We want our children to like us and we want their friends to like us. It's a mistake. Parents need to deliver messages from time to time that are unpopular. In fact, parenting is not a popular role very often. If you are more concerned about being liked by your children than you are about being a good parent, your ability to successfully challenge and correct them in ways that they need to be challenged and corrected is likely to be seriously compromised.

2. *Children need heroes and mentors.* The best way to encourage them in the direction of great heroes and mentors is to have great ones yourself. We are all fascinated with the stories of other men and woman who have done extraordinary things with their lives, or ordinary things in an extraordinary way or with extraordinary love. Be careful who you look up to and champion, your children are paying attention.

You may be able to distinguish between the incredible musical genius of your favorite artist and his questionable lifestyle of sex, drugs, and alcohol . . . but chances are your children don't or can't make the distinction. You walk into the bedrooms of most adolescents and see the posters they have hanging on their walls, and you know they are becoming like the people on the posters . . . and that is frightening.

We all need heroes. Who are yours? Do you want your children to grow up to be like them? If not, it might be time to find some new heroes. Celebrate who and what you want your children to grow to be and become. We become what we celebrate.

3. *More than anything else, your children need your time.* Some may argue that they need love more than they need time, but time is one of the greatest external proofs of the internal mystery we call love. I can say I love you, but it is an internal mystery. You don't really know I love you until I act out of that love. If I said I loved you but never wanted to spend any time with you, you would quickly begin to question my love, and rightfully so. I was having lunch a few months ago with some new friends in California, and they asked me what I was writing. I explained that I was working on a book about families. Tim and Mike started to share stories about their families and the triumphs and trials of parenting, and at the end of our discussion Tim turned to me and said, "The one thing that Mike and I have discovered as fathers, and we talk about it all the time, is that it's just easier to parent a child when you are there."

It's just easier to parent a child when you are there. Parenting requires time, enormous amounts of time. You cannot expect your child to report on his day the way your direct reports at work do—in rapid fire because they have only three minutes. Your child can tell you about her day in three minutes, but she won't tell you the most important stuff. She will skim the surface to satisfy your question. You will go away patting yourself on the back for talking to your child and think all is well, but who knows what is really going on inside your child's heart and mind. Most of us don't spill our guts when someone asks how we are. We need to be convinced that the other person really wants to know how we are before we reveal ourselves—and that takes time.

Children hunger for their parents' time. When they are young they want to be with you, be around you, be near you. Encourage that. Make time for that, because soon enough they will be asserting their independence in so many ways. Form the habit of spending time together before that happens, so that when they are going through those difficult times of adolescence, it doesn't seem so forced and unnatural when you spend time with them.

They want your time. They need your time. It is easy to get caught up in lots of things that may seem urgent but are certainly not more important. A friend conveyed a story to me recently that powerfully conveys the point.

A man came home from work late, tired and irritated to find his five-year-old son waiting for him at the door.
  "Daddy, may I ask you a question?"
  "Yeah, sure, what is it?" replied the man.
  "Daddy, how much money do you make an hour?"

"That's none of your business, what makes you ask such a thing?" the man said angrily.

"I just want to know. Please tell me, how much do you make an hour?" pleaded the little boy.

"If you must know, I make twenty dollars an hour."

"Oh," the little boy replied, head bowed. Then, looking up, he said, "Daddy, may I borrow ten dollars, please?"

The father was furious. "If the only reason you want to know how much money I make is just so you can borrow some to buy a silly toy or some other nonsense, then you march yourself straight to your room and go to bed. Think about why you're being so selfish. I work long, hard hours every day and don't have time for such childish games."

The little boy quietly went to his room and shut the door. The man sat down and started to get even madder about the little boy's questioning. How dare he ask such questions only to get some money. After an hour or so, the man had calmed down, and started to think he may have been a little hard on his son. Maybe there was something he really needed to buy with that ten dollars, and he really didn't ask for money very often. The man went to the door of the little boy's room and opened the door. "Are you asleep, son?" he asked.

"No, Daddy, I'm awake," replied the boy.

"I've been thinking, maybe I was too hard on you earlier," said the man. "It's been a long day, and I took my aggravation out on you. Here's that ten dollars you asked for."

The little boy sat straight up beaming. "Oh, thank you, Daddy!" he yelled. Then, reaching under his pillow, he pulled out some more crumpled-up bills. The man, seeing that the boy already had money started to get angry again.

The little boy slowly counted out the money, then looked up at the man.

"Why did you want more money if you already had some?" the father asked.

"Because I didn't have enough, but I do now," the little boy replied. "Daddy, I have twenty dollars now . . . Can I buy an hour of your time?"

We give our time to who and what we love. Children yearn for the time of their parents. In a world where we are pulled in so many directions, finding the time to spend with our children is perhaps the greatest challenge facing parents today. This is why it is so important to know what matters most and what we are really about. The only way to say no to something is to have a deeper yes. We have to constantly assert that spending time with our children is a deeper yes. Otherwise, we will be accosted on a daily basis and carried away from our families by the seemingly urgent things. There are many urgent things in our lives each day, but the most important things are hardly ever urgent. That's why we need to identify them, give them priority, and place them at the center of our lives.

4. *Children need to develop a strong sense of self.* By this I mean children need to know who they are and what they are here for. You may argue that many adults don't know this, how can we expect children to develop it? It is in fact considerably easier to develop during childhood and adolescence than it is during adulthood. Your next question is probably, "How do I help my child to develop a strong sense of self?"

Teach and encourage them to develop and nurture their spiritual side. Most people are very uncomfortable in silence and solitude. For this reason, they have to be around people all the time and have noise on all the time. Teach your child to be comfortable in her own company, to enjoy his own company. Once we are comfortable in our own company we learn to walk away from many people and situations in our lives. Until we are comfortable in our own company we are at the mercy of our peer group and wherever they may lead us. It is not necessarily that we love being with them as much as it is that we cannot stand to be alone. In each day, give a place in your life to silence and solitude.

The other way to nurture a child's spiritual side is to encourage her to listen to the voice of God in her life. The happiest people I know are those with a sense of mission in their lives, and we don't choose a mission, we are called. But you cannot be called if you aren't listening. Ask your child: "What is God saying to you today?" The first time they may look at you a little strange, but the second time they will have an answer. Simply asking the question will lead them to start listening.

5. *Your children need your love.* Love them. It seems so simple and obvious, but in the hustle and bustle of our everyday lives, it is easy to neglect. Parenting is about a love of self-donation—the giving of our self for the life of another. Yes, we donate money to our favorite charity and we donate our old clothes to the goodwill store, but parenting requires that we donate our very self.

Just the other day I was thinking to myself, "When was the last time you did something just completely out of love, detached from self-interest, just completely and purely out of love?" I had to think for a minute, and I didn't like that. It's a simple thing, but not an easy thing. We are all capable of it and it is the only thing that really changes things—love. The only thing that changes *things* is love. Not power, not war, not money, not fame—love. Love is the change dynamic in history. Love transforms people, relationships, workplaces, families, communities, nations . . . In fact, there is nothing that love does not transform.

Our children need to know that they are loved. Not because they are cute or because they did well in school, not because they did what we asked them, and not even because they are our children. They need to know that they are loved independent of anything they say or do. They need to know that no matter what happens, they will always be loved. It is this detached love, which seeks to liberate rather than control, that sets children free to be and become all they were created to be.

Children don't need the latest running shoes and high-tech gadgets. These things are so easy to give them. What children genuinely need is fairly simple when we step back and gain perspective. And that perspective reminds us that if we just spend time with our children, much of the rest will begin to happen spontaneously and naturally. By the time the average American child is six, he has spent more time watching television than he will spend talking to his father throughout his entire life. Doing something about this is a way for every parent to change the world.

What Are You Willing to Sacrifice?

Everything comes at a cost. You cannot play golf and tennis at the same time, so playing golf comes at the cost of playing tennis. It is a simple example, but every day we make choices that exclude other options. In economics we call this opportunity cost. If you want to have a great marriage, you can, but it will come at a cost. If you want to be a great parent, you can, but it will come at a cost. Our culture tells us we can have it all, but that is a lie. By saying yes to some things, you necessarily say no to others.

Parenting by its very nature is a sacrifice. There is no question that parenting has a great many joys and rewards, but it also comes at a cost and requires significant sacrifices. When you get married, you have to start thinking about how everything you do or plan will affect another person. Before you schedule certain things you have to talk with your husband or wife to compare personal and professional schedules and preferences with each other. As a single person, when your friends asked if you wanted to go skiing for the weekend, the only person you needed to consult was yourself, but in marriage there is another person to think of. In a similar way, but on a whole new level, when you have a child, you have to constantly think about how what you do or plan will affect your newborn child. Something as simple as listening to the radio at outrageously loud volumes has all sorts of implications. One of the things parents seem constantly called to sacrifice is their preferences. You may prefer to listen to loud music, but your child is sleeping. You may prefer one thing for lunch, but your children want something else. You may prefer to sleep in on a Saturday morning, but your children are up at the crack of dawn. Any of these may seem small on their own, but after adding dozens and dozens of them together every day, the sacrifice becomes real and significant.

In the case of a child, unlike the marriage scenario, the child is completely helpless and totally dependent upon you. People mourn their loss of independence in marriage with the birth of their first child, and for good reason. In fact, it is very healthy to mourn this loss. Mourning this loss of independence helps us to make the transition to a new way of living. There are those who hold on desperately to their old way of life. Those who don't mourn this loss of independence often live in denial, refuse to acknowledge it, and cause tremendous anxiety to themselves and strain to their relationships.

Parenting involves real sacrifices. Most parents are willing to make enormous sacrifices for their children. We do it out of love. We do it because we want our children to have a life as good as our own, in many cases better than our own. We do it for the joy of parenting, for the sheer satisfaction of knowing that we are helping our child, flesh of our flesh, grow, learn, and discover the world.

When we speak of self-donation, giving oneself, parents do it in a way that is awesomely consistent. Every day they die unto themselves in a thousand little ways so their children can thrive. Most of the ways parents deny their own preferences for the sake of their children go unnoticed. It is a thankless job a lot of the time, sometimes for years on end. So, how can we approach this sacrifice in a healthy way? Two of the keys are a good sense of humor and a clear understanding of purpose.

Keep always in the forefront of your mind your own purpose—to become the-best-version-of-yourself. Every moment of parenting provides you with an opportunity to grow and become a-better-version-of-yourself. When you have to make sacrifices for your children, don't just do it because you have to. Make it count. Harness the hidden power of those sacrifices. Each sacrifice you have to make, each time you have to abandon your own preferences, every time you have to die unto yourself so that your children can live more abundantly is an opportunity to grow in virtue. Patience, fortitude, generosity, self-possession . . . these are the fruits of your sacrifices. Cherish them. Celebrate them. We will never make it unless we learn to see the sacrifices love demands of us as a way to become the-best-version-of-ourselves, and to help our children do the same.

So we have established that parenting involves a great many sacrifices, but there is another question for us to consider. Is it possible to sacrifice too much? The answer is, absolutely. It happens all the time and always ends ugly.

The reality is that you have needs, too. You may be a parent, but you are still a person and have legitimate needs in the same four areas as your children do—physical, emotional, intellectual, and spiritual.

Your legitimate needs are fairly simple, but that doesn't mean they are easy to satisfy. Physically, you need regular exercise, a balanced diet, and sufficient sleep. Emotionally, you need opportunities to love and be loved, and carefree time-lessness with your children and spouse. Intellectually, you need opportunities to stimulate and nourish your mind. Spir-itually, you need silence and solitude.

A quick examination reveals that your needs are very sim-ilar to your children's legitimate needs, only you have all the responsibilities of being an adult and a parent competing for your time. Our lives are so full and are moving at such an alarming pace that something as simple as regular exercise can be a real challenge for the modern parent.

The first step is to identify your legitimate needs and to ask your spouse to do the same. Once you have identified these, it is helpful to make a commitment to yourself and to each other that your needs come before your wants. Defending your needs may require you to make tough choices profes-sionally and socially. At times, you may have to give up what you really want in order to honor what you really need, but over time, if you honor and respect your legitimate needs, you will get more and more of what you want. When we de-fend and celebrate our legitimate needs, we begin to thrive, and this thriving produces extraordinary results in all areas of our lives.

Most of us believe this to be true when we step back and consider it, but very few of us have the self-possession to delay our gratification. Yet isn't that exactly the discipline that leads to the success we are trying to instill in our children?

You may simply say, "*Impossible*. There is no way I could work out three times a week!" Impossible is a large word and should be used with great caution. It's possible, but it will re-quire real effort. I was speaking last week with Kathy, a woman who attended one of my retreats where I discussed these ideas. Kathy and her husband, Mike, then proceeded to identify their legitimate needs and discovered that her need for exercise had really been neglected. They then made an agreement that two nights a week, when he got home from work, he would take care of the children while she went to the gym. A third afternoon, they agreed to hire a babysitter so that she could go to the gym three times a week. This required adjustments to their schedules, their lifestyles, and their budget. But twelve months later they could not be happier that they made the change. Kathy said, "I am so much happier, and you can't tell me that's not good for my kids and my husband. So we don't go out to eat as much, but I just feel less frantic. I have that time to be by myself and to really work out some of the stress of my days, and I know I am a better mother and a better wife. In fact, I am a better person, and that's no small thing."

The fulfillment of our legitimate needs is not usually something we can just do on our own. If you are a single parent, as we have already discussed, this presents unique challenges and this is one of the areas. Regular exercise can be a challenge of monumental proportions and requires real planning. Who are your partners? Perhaps your parents can watch your child (or children) a couple of times a week, maybe you have a neighbor who can help out, or perhaps you can afford a babysitter on a regular basis to make this happen. Whatever way you approach it, your legitimate needs are important.

The next thing for us to consider is when it is all right to neglect our legitimate needs because of the needs of our children or our spouse. In the case of both—children and spouse—we should be willing to put their needs ahead of our needs. We should be much less willing to put their wants before our needs. And even when we are required to put the needs of our children or spouse in front of our needs, it should not be for an indefinite period of time. For example, when a woman gives birth to a child, she knows that she is in for many sleepless nights during the child's infancy. However, she knows this will not go on forever. Eventually infants sleep through the night and mothers are once again able to enjoy a full and uninterrupted night's sleep. The same may be true in caring for a spouse who is recovering from an operation. For days, sometimes even weeks, you may have to forgo some of your real and legitimate needs, but this should not be an indefinite situation. If a situation like this stretches on for more than a few weeks, it is critically important that we return to attending to our own real and legitimate needs. Taking care of ourselves in this way is part of our responsibility to our spouse. In this situation it may be necessary to reach out to other people in our lives to partner with us in order for us to care for a sick or recovering spouse while at the same time attending to our legitimate needs.

One scenario that we should be particularly mindful of is when our spouse or child (usually an adult child) continually puts his or her needs (and often wants) ahead of our needs. This is particularly common with people suffering from addiction, whether it be alcohol, gambling, or drugs. An addict thinks only of him- or herself. Everything must be as they want it otherwise they become irritable, restless, and discontent. They will often come to loved ones and say, "I need you to do this . . . or that. . . ." These are often false needs, but because we love them so much we begin to neglect our real needs to give them what they claim they need, or simply to keep the peace. The real test here is whether or not there is an end in sight. A mother can go without sleep because she is given special grace and can see the end in sight. Often in situations of addiction, dysfunction, and codependency, those we love ask us directly or indirectly to give up some of our legitimate needs with no end in sight. This is not healthy—for you or for them.

Understanding the difference between needs and wants is one of the great lessons you can teach your children in a real and practical way every day. Teaching your children to respect your legitimate needs is a powerful way to equip your children for strong and dynamic relationships founded on mutual respect. Failing to teach our children about our legitimate needs as parents will lead them to constantly assert their wants ahead of our needs and will inevitably create selfish children.

Your children have legitimate needs, your spouse has legitimate needs, but so do you. Your needs should be honored at every turn, if not by others then at least by yourself. If love requires you to neglect one or many of your legitimate needs it should only ever be temporary. And we should be wary of putting other people's wants ahead of our needs.

Dreams and Fears

Two of the most powerful forces at work in the life of a human being are dreams and fears, and they both emerge from within us. They also provide a unique opportunity to create real bonds of intimacy with those we love.

Our culture thinks that sex and intimacy are the same thing. They are not. I cannot tell you how many people have come up to me over the years and told me that they have read all of my books except *The Seven Levels of Intimacy* because they thought it was a book about sex. Sex is not intimacy. Intimacy is the process of mutual self-revelation. Intimacy is you and me revealing ourselves to each other, and this takes place in all our relationships to varying extents and on different levels. But to develop a real intimacy with our children should be a goal as parents, and dreams and fears are at the heart of this intimacy.

In the area of dreams, the first thing we need to recognize as parents is that we have dreams for our children. Beyond the one word to perfectly describe your child in the future, parents have a myriad of dreams for their children. Some of them are spoken and others are hidden away in the recesses of our hearts and minds. But even the unspoken dreams we hold for our children have a way of influencing the way we raise them.

What are your dreams for your children? If it helps, take out a piece of paper and write them down: to be a doctor, a lawyer, a baseball player . . . to find someone worthy of their love and have a wonderful marriage . . . to find work they can be passionate about . . . to make a lot of money . . . to be successful . . . to travel the world . . .

There could be dozens, even hundreds of them. But as wonderful as all these dreams are, you have to realize that they are *your* dreams for your children. Your children will have their own dreams. What's important is not that your children live your dreams, but that they discover and live their own dreams. Your dreams may be good and noble, but that still doesn't make them their dreams, and it is the dreams deep within them that hold the map of their life just as it is meant to be. If you over assert your dreams for their lives you will rob them of their unique journey and make it almost impossible for them to be happy. The dreams parents have for their children have a unique power over their children. Even long after our parents are dead we tend to be heavily influenced, often unconsciously, by the dreams they had for us. Tread lightly when it comes to verbalizing your dreams for your children, you may short-circuit their ability to dream for themselves.

One of the most amazing things parents can do for their children is to help them live their dreams. The connection that is made between people who help each other live their dreams is phenomenal. We love the people who help us chase down and accomplish our dreams.

I have often spoken about my Dream Book. In it, I jot down places I would like to go, books I would like to write, qualities I would like to develop in my character and relationships, things I'd like to buy, things I'd like to experience, and on and on. So many of my dreams seemed impossible when I first wrote them in my Dream Book, but today the dreams that seemed impossible seem so small. As we chase down and accomplish our dreams, we dream bigger dreams. This process is powerful in the life of a person, and especially a child. If you can teach your child to identify his or her dreams and then work to achieve them, there is almost no field they will not succeed in.

This is one of the most powerful abilities we have and one of the most unemployed. Our unique ability as human beings to look into the future, imagine a better state of affairs, and then act in the present moment to create that future reality is nothing short of extraordinary. Teaching our children to engage and exercise this ability is one of life's greatest lessons.

Many parents are afraid to encourage their children to dream because they fear their children will fail. This leads us into the second great motivator: fear. And one of our greatest fears is the fear of failure. I have recently noticed in my work in schools that more and more young people are paralyzed by the fear of failure. There is such an emphasis on success, and they are so afraid of failing, that they simply do not get involved in anything that they are not required to. This fear of failure is, as best I can tell, a great shift in the American spirit. The greatness of America was built by men and women who were willing to try and fail as often as it took to get it right. But with the overemphasis on test scores, and excelling in all subjects and areas, we are breeding this willingness to try and fail out of our children. The implications for our culture could be monumental, and if this is not stemmed in the not too distant future, America will be overtaken in all sorts of arenas by the young minds of other nations who are simply willing to try and fail.

We need to remind our children that it is okay to fail. There are plenty of cultural examples to draw from. If you have a batting average of 300 in baseball you are one of the best. What does this say? It says that if you fail 70 percent of the time in baseball, you are one of the great players. In golf, if you win one out of every ten golf tournaments you enter, you will find yourself among the best. These are the numbers that our young people need to be made aware of in order to free them from the paralyzing fear of failure. Instead, we bombard them with the overwhelming successes of so many people in so many arenas that we create in them the false belief that it is not okay to fail. Nothing grows in the shade of great trees. Our young people need to be encouraged to get out into the arena of life and try, and fail, confident in the knowledge that trying and failing is part of the wonderful learning process we call life.

If your child does not have some really good failures under his or her belt by the time you send them off to college, this is a cause for concern, because failure is an inevitable part of life. And learning to deal with failure is an indispensable part of success in all we do.

Beyond the fear of failure, it is important to recognize that children have a lot of fears. As they grow into adolescents and consider the prospect of fending for themselves in the world, their fears multiply and their ability to recognize what is happening to them is almost nonexistent. One of the best ways to recognize the role fear plays in the lives of our children (and even our spouse and friends and colleagues) is to examine our own fears. Consider the question: What is the most dominant emotion in our society today? The answer of course is fear. We are afraid of certain parts of town. We are afraid of certain types of people. We are afraid we will lose our jobs. We are afraid we won't have enough money to retire. We are afraid of terrorists. We are afraid of changing weather conditions. We are afraid of what type of world we are bringing our children into. People are afraid they won't find the right person to spend their lives with. Others are afraid they will fail at marriage. We are afraid our children will fail at marriage. We are afraid we will get sick. We are afraid we won't have health insurance. We are afraid of losing things we have worked hard to buy. We are afraid of rejection. We are afraid of failure. We are afraid of criticism, suffering, heartache. We are afraid of so many things, and all this fear is powerfully impacting our lives and our relationships.

But there is one fear that dominates the human landscape, one fear that we all share. We are afraid that if people really knew us they would no longer love us. This is what stops us from revealing ourselves to others, and children, particularly as they approach adolescence, are in many cases completely ruled by this fear. Their desire for acceptance is so great that they will alter the very DNA of their personality and ignore the good and noble voice within them in order to fit in and be accepted.

This is where making yourself vulnerable makes you a great leader and great parent. In the process of self-revelation someone always has to go first. Are you willing to share your dreams and fears with your children? Not your dreams and fears for them but your own dreams and fears. By making yourself vulnerable in this way you teach them many lessons and create a tremendous bond, but it has to be sincere, otherwise they will see through it in about ten seconds.

When you speak about your dreams, speak about dreams

that are realistic and achievable but will also stretch and challenge you. If you are a forty-year-old father of three and you talk about a dream of playing Major League Baseball, you will teach your children that dreaming is about fantasies that are impossible to accomplish. If you only speak about broken dreams of the past, you will teach your children that dreaming is a waste of time and only leads to broken hearts and crushed sprits. Don't talk to your children about a dream unless you are committed to making an earnest effort to accomplish that dream. Otherwise they will see you as a hypocrite who talks a good game but confines himself to the bench, and worse yet, they will think that it is enough just to talk about our dreams. It is one thing if they see you dream and try and fail. It is something completely different if they hear you talking about your dreams but never see you making an earnest attempt to accomplish them.

In the same way, when you talk about your fears, remember it is about what *you* fear not what you fear *for them*. You don't want to scare your children by telling them about your fears. You don't want to burden them with your fears before they are able to carry such a burden. You simply want to awaken them to the fact that you have fears, that it's okay to have fears, and that fears don't need to paralyze us. In this area, it can be very helpful to talk about fears you had in the past that you worried and worried about, but that turned out to be nothing at all. This can be a powerful lesson about the futility of worry and can help you to communicate to your children that most of the things we worry about never actually happen.

Dreams animate us. They bring us to life by breathing passion, energy, purpose, and enthusiasm into our days and lives. Dreams lead us to explore the upper reaches of the-best-version-of-ourselves. Fear paralyzes us. Fears causes us to draw back from life rather than embrace life as a marvelous adventure. Fear has a tremendous ability to prevent us from becoming the-best-version-of-ourselves if we allow it to rule our psyche.

We are driven by our dreams and our fears. Which is winning in your life? Which do you want to dominate the lives of your children?

What Are the Best Things You Can Do for Your Children?

Talking to people who are struggling in their marriages, you discover they all have different problems, but you also discover that there are two things they all have in common. They don't communicate well and they don't have enough time together alone (that is, without their children). The former of course requires and thrives on the latter. All relationships thrive when we feed them with carefree timelessness. That's why young people fall in love so easily—carefree timelessness. They have all this time just to discover each other. The rest of us fall out of love so easily because we starve our relationships of the carefree timelessness that caused them to thrive in the first place.

When I look at marriages that seem to be really working, I find that some of the biggest differences are in the way they approach time and communication. They spend time with each other without their children on a regular basis. They go out together regularly without their children, not to run errands or to a function, but just to catch up and enjoy each other. They go away overnight from time to time alone, even if it's just to a hotel a couple of towns over. They have a regular time in their day when they talk, either on the phone, in person, or both—and it is not at the end of the day when they are both exhausted and don't have the energy for the really tough discussions. They are committed to working on their communication skills regardless of the fact that they are way ahead of the game and better than most. It might be helpful to reflect on each of these five habits and consider how well you are doing with each.

As we have already discussed, both children and parents have real and legitimate needs and one of the great challenges in the life of a family is to balance the needs of the children and the needs of the parents. To neglect either is to misstep. But because the needs of our children are so apparent, and because we have difficulty differentiating sometimes between their needs and wants, and because we want to give them the best life we can, and because many of us feel guilty about doing things for ourselves . . . it is easy for a marriage to be kidnapped by the children. But not only children kidnap marriages. Work can just as easily kidnap a marriage, as can friends, social involvement, and any number of other things. But in our day and age, it seems that children are directing the daily course of events in families more than ever before.

I think this is the time for us to pause and consider what are the best things we can do for our children. Is it providing them with the best education available? Is it saving and investing diligently in order to give them a good start in life, or leave them an inheritance? Is it showing them the world through a variety of travel experiences? Or is it perhaps exposing them to the right opportunities and people so they can have a successful career in their chosen field?

We focus quite a bit on these areas, and other things like them, but these are not the best things parents can do for their children. They are wonderful and exciting, but they are secondary. These are the three best things you can do for your children as a parent.

1. *Dedicate yourself to becoming a-better-version-of-yourself each and every day.* The writer James Baldwin observed, "Children have never been very good at listening to their elders, but they have never failed to imitate them." Whatever it is you wish to teach your children—live it! The best way we can encourage them to fully embrace the dream of becoming the-best-version-of-themselves is to walk that path ourselves. If they see that working out is a part of your lifestyle, it will become part of theirs. If they see you fueling your body with foods that are healthy, it will become part of their lives. If they see you spending quality time with your spouse, it will become part of their lives. If they see you taking quiet time each day for prayer and reflection, it will become part of their lives. The best thing you can do for your children is to strive to become the-best-version-of-yourself. It is also the

best thing you can do for your spouse, significant other, friends, company, church, nation, and humanity. When we become more perfectly ourselves, everyone who crosses our path forever will benefit from that growth.

2. *Live with passion and purpose.* If you ask parents if they want their children to grow up to live passionate and purposeful lives they will say, "Absolutely!" But how many parents are living passionate and purposeful lives? Not so many. I am not talking about doing extraordinary things in extraordinary ways. I am speaking of approaching ordinary things with passion and purpose.

I don't work hard because I will lose my job if I don't, and I don't work hard because I get paid to. I work hard because working hard and paying attention to the details of my work helps me to become a-better-version-of-myself. In this way, my work has a purpose way beyond money or advancement or survival. When I approach my work in this way, and I must admit I do not every day, but when I do I am living purposefully. Nothing is more ordinary than work, but it can be done purposefully.

Similarly, what are your passions? Are you passionate about learning, music, art, travel, science, investing? Have you allowed your parenting and career to crowd out your passions? When our children see us pursuing and enjoying our passions, they begin to consider what they themselves are passionate about—and through their passions, one of life's great adventures begins.

Living passionately and purposefully is one of the greatest gifts parents can give their children.

3. *Have a great marriage.* I realize that 50 percent of the people who read this book will likely be divorced or single parents. At the same time, I think most people—married, divorced, single, or separated—can agree that the best scenario would be for children to be raised in the context of a great marriage. Yet it's not always possible, so we do the best we can with what we have, but that doesn't mean we should stop celebrating the ideal.

One of the best things you can do for your children is to have a great marriage. When two people love each other, encourage and challenge each other to become the-best-version-of-themselves, and honor and respect each other's individual journey while at the same time dynamically collaborating on their journey together, it produces a rare energy and environment. Anyone fortunate enough to wander into this environment for an afternoon or an entire childhood will benefit enormously. A great marriage is a place where we can be ourselves, a refuge from the world, and a place where we can grow through both harmony and conflict. Marriage is a place where we can be comforted and challenged, a place where dreams are explored and pursued, and a place where ego can be tamed and true self can blossom.

Your marriage is not something separate from your parenting. It is an integral part of it. Your marriage is the life source of your parenting. The daily regimen of parenting proposes an endless number of things to be done. The important word here is endless. Even if you got everything done that you thought fulfilled your role as a parent today, you would discover that there are still an endless number of things you could do for your child. That is never going to change. You could dedicate your whole life to helping your children grow and succeed in this world. Urgent things often dominate the life of a parent. We rush around doing urgent things all day long. The problem with this, of course, is that the most important things are hardly ever urgent. That is why it is so important for us to identify what the most important things are and place them at the center of our lives by giving them priority. Striving to become a-better-version-of-yourself is one of the most life-giving things we can give our time, focus, and energy to, but it will never be urgent. Living passionately and purposefully is never urgent, it can always be put off for one more day—and people put it off for a whole lifetime while they obsess over all the urgent stuff. In the same way, having a great marriage will never be urgent. If we needed a great marriage to survive in the same way we need air to breathe and water to drink, I suspect there would be a lot more great marriages around. But it is not urgent, and as such, too easy to put off for another day or another year.

The best things we can do for our children are almost never urgent. For this reason, from time to time we need to step away from all the seemingly urgent things in order to discover and attend to the things that matter most.

Tough but Fair

For almost a decade now I have been in the habit of asking people about the teachers, coaches, and mentors they most respect and admire. The stories that people share in response to this question are many and varied. They are inspiring and remind us of the powerful influence one person can have on our lives. And yet, as unique and individual as the stories are to the people telling them, there also seems to be a common thread. When they get to telling me about the teacher or coach they are most grateful for, I then like to ask them, "How would you describe his or her style?" Almost inevitably the answer is the same: tough but fair. They may say it in a different way or use different words, but in essence it comes down to the same thing.

In my corporate work, I use this example to explain to managers that in order to gain the respect of employees or those who report to them, we must be tough but fair. If you give a pay raise to someone who has done a poor job, you encourage the wrong behavior, you weaken your business and its ability to perform, but perhaps most of all you weaken the team because you lose respect as a leader, which diminishes your ability to manage and lead, which in turn jeopardizes the future of the venture.

Successful parenting is as much about gaining and keeping the respect of our children. It is important to point out that respect is not the same as popularity. In fact, in many cases, in order to assure respect way into the future, we must be willing to surrender popularity in the present.

At the very core of leadership, management, parenting, and love is the approach of tough but fair. If you are too easy on them and let them do whatever they want, they won't respect you because they will see you as a pushover. If you are too hard on them and never let them exercise their free will and preferences, they will see you as unreasonable and un-bending and you will lose their respect that way.

Tough but fair means holding them accountable. We all need to be accountable to someone. It brings out the best in us. People do not do well in situations where they are not accountable to anyone or anything. In fact, the absence of accountability inevitably leads to our spinning out of control. The framers knew this as well as anybody. The Founding Fathers had unique insight into the very nature of the human being when they wrote: "All men are created equal, that they are endowed by their Creator with certain unalienable Rights, that among these are Life, Liberty, and the pursuit of happiness." But the framers also displayed profound insight into human nature in writing the Constitution when they set up a series of checks and balances in order to avoid a situation where someone would have power without accountability.

Accountability does not stifle us; it brings out the best in us. Whether you are managing people in the workplace or raising your children, your role demands that you hold them accountable. Our attempts to hold our children accountable will be most successful if we are able to clearly define for them a vision toward which we are parenting. If you are able to tell your children that you love them and that you want to help them become the-best-version-of-themselves, and that you consider that to be your role as a parent, when an issue arises you can speak to the issue by celebrating the vision. You can also let them know that as a parent you feel it is your responsibility to be tough but fair. At times they may think you are being too tough—and you should carefully consider with your partner whether or not that is the case. At other times they may claim you are not being fair. There is certainly not a parent on the planet who has not heard that cry. At the end of the day you can only do what you believe to be best. Sometimes you will get it wrong. When you realize that you got it wrong, apologize to your children. At the heart of great parenting is a deep humility that we have been entrusted with an awesome role and tremendous responsibility.

When the Native American people make a decision for their community they ask the question: "How will what we are considering affect our people seven generations from now?" In raising our children it is all too easy to get caught up in the here and now. Parenting is a leadership role, and leaders look beyond the here and now to consider the pros and cons at various times in the future. If we genuinely want to serve our children's best interests we must find within ourselves the courage to be tough but fair in our dealings with them, to hold them accountable. This courage is born from a vision of what we wish to achieve through our parenting. By clearly establishing the goals of our parenting we are given the courage to parent to that vision.

It goes without saying that this tough but fair approach would be interwoven with a deep love for our children, daily encouragement and support, and an open and understanding heart.

Parenting in the twenty-first century is no easy proposition. We are busy because the world is busier, and the busier the world gets the more time it takes to parent successfully. Here in this section we have laid out a plan. Let's review briefly.

Clearly establish what you are trying to achieve. Know what success looks like. Very few good things happen by accident, they are usually the result of a well-thought-out and executed plan.

Be aware that you are a leader. Study other great leaders in a variety of areas in life. Develop the traits that are responsible for their success. Learn to apply them to your parenting.

Know what you should and should not be willing to sacrifice in order to help your children become the-best-version-of-themselves.

Determine what your children's legitimate needs are, but also become intimately aware of your own needs.

Acknowledge the powerful role dreams and fears play in our lives.

Focus on the most important things, not just the urgent things.

Parent toward your vision. Beware of parenting to be popular. Adopt a tough but fair approach to decisions in order to hold your children accountable.

Parenting is difficult. To begin with, any other conception is to massively deceive ourselves and set ourselves up for much confusion and frustration. Much of our unhappiness is caused by the gap that exists between what we think will happen and what actually happens. Our own expectations create a great deal of the unhappiness in our lives. We should approach parenting as though it is going to be difficult, but are unlikely to have that expectation disappointed. But for all the struggles and heartaches that come with parenting, there is a joy that cannot be described or suppressed. I recently read the following anonymous passage, which seems to aptly capture the essence of the role.

POSITION AVAILABLE. *Must be willing to be hated, at least temporarily, until someone needs $5. Must be willing to bite tongue repeatedly. Also, must possess the physical stamina of a pack mule and be able to go from zero to 60 mph in three seconds flat in case, this time, the screams from the backyard are not someone just crying wolf. Must be willing to face stimulating technical challenges, such as small gadget repair, mysteriously sluggish toilets, and stuck zippers. Must screen phone calls, maintain calendars, and coordinate production of multiple homework projects. Must have ability to plan and organize social gatherings for clients of all ages and mental outlooks. Must be willing to be indispensable one minute, an embarrassment the next. Must handle assembly and product safety testing of a half million cheap, plastic toys and battery-operated devices. Must always hope for the best but be prepared for the worst. Must assume final, complete accountability for the quality of the end product. Responsibilities also include floor maintenance and janitorial work throughout the facility.*
POSSIBILITY FOR ADVANCEMENT & PROMOTION: *None. Your job is to remain in the same position for years, without complaining, constantly retraining and updating your skills, so that those in your charge can ultimately surpass you.*
PREVIOUS EXPERIENCE: *None required, unfortunately. On-the-job training offered on a continually exhausting basis.*

WAGES AND COMPENSATION: *Get this! You pay them! Offering frequent raises and bonuses. A balloon payment is due when they turn 18 because of the assumption that college will help them become financially independent. When you die, you give them whatever is left. The oddest thing about this reverse-salary scheme is that you actually enjoy it and wish you could only do more.*

BENEFITS: *While no health or dental insurance, no pension, no tuition reimbursement, no paid holidays, and no stock options are offered, this job supplies limitless opportunities for personal growth and free hugs and kisses for life if you play your cards right.*

Now, let's explore some of the practical ways we can approach parenting in order to raise amazing children.

4

Raising Amazing Children

The deepest desire in a parent's heart is to see one's child grow to live a life filled with happiness, yet rarely do we realize and consciously acknowledge that the most direct way to that happiness is by celebrating and defending the-best-version-of-ourselves. Consider some of the activities that help you to become a better-version-of-yourself. You know they will bring a lasting happiness to your life in the midst of a changing world, and yet often you still struggle to choose them and give them priority in your life. If we take the physical realm as an example, we all know that regular exercise and a balanced diet help us to become a-better-version-of-ourselves and bring a certain happiness to our lives, but we often resist. When it is time to work out we can find a thousand excuses and reasons why we can't, or shouldn't, or don't want to, but when we get done working out we are always glad we did. This is the struggle your children are in. In every moment, like yourself, they are choosing between the-best-version-of-themselves and some other second-rate version. As a parent, you cannot control them, but you can help them, guide them, assist them, inspire them, encourage them, challenge them, and gently lead them in the direction of a life lived to the fullest.

One of the ways you can exert enormous influence with

your children is through the culture you create as a leader for your family. In this section we are going to examine some of the ways you can create a culture that helps your children to discover and celebrate their best selves.

Ask the Right Questions

I have had the pleasure of working with some great leaders in both the corporate and nonprofit sectors, and one trait I have noticed that they all tend to share is that they know how to ask the right questions. Parents are always asking me, "What can I say to my children to get them to . . . ?" We often seem to obsess over what we are going to say to children, when in fact we need to shift our focus and instead listen to what they have to say to us. They are, however, unlikely to just come into the room and start talking. We need to develop the art of drawing them out, and the right question will turn to conversation every time. At other times we need to be able to use the right questions to get young people to think about themselves and their lives in a way that is different from the perspectives they get from their friends or the culture.

It is fascinating to me that if a five- or six-year-old child comes to you and asks "Can I do this?" or "Can I have that?," and you in turn ask them "Will it help you become the-best-version-of-yourself?," they know instantly. Even if the child has never heard the phrase before, if he or she is old enough to understand the concept, the child knows instantly. The reason is because this dream is already within them, and within you and me. The idea of becoming the-best-version-of-yourself is not something I am trying to impose upon you. I am simply trying to draw it out of you. In the same way, you don't need to impose it upon your children. It's already within them. Your role is simply to draw it out. Questions can play a powerful role in helping children discover the-best-version-of-themselves.

Life is as much about the questions we ask as it is about the answers we find. In fact, the questions we ask of life are more important than the answers we find, because if you ask the wrong questions you always get the wrong answers. This is one of the serious defects of the modern popular culture that today's young people find themselves immersed in. The problem in our society today is that we are asking all the wrong questions.

Raising amazing children is first and foremost about asking the right questions of ourselves, our spouses, and our children. Throughout this book we have been asking: What is the one word you would use to describe your child when your role as a parent is done? What is your vision for this person? What is your vision of family?

These are the questions on which I based this book. It would have been a very different book if I had used other questions, like: Should children be allowed to divorce their parents? Should a fourteen-year-old girl be able to have an abortion without the knowledge of her parents? Should gay couples be able to adopt children? I didn't choose these questions. The questions I have based this book upon are primary questions. These others are secondary questions. The way you answer secondary questions spring from your visions for the human person and the family. All the disagreements that go on around these secondary questions is because we have differing visions for the human person and family.

There is an art to asking the right questions and every parent should learn the art. Let me share some ordinary everyday examples with you.

Your ten-year-old son, Johnny, comes home from school and says, "Mom, can I watch television before I do my homework?" Now, you can deal with that in several ways. You can say, "Sure, Johnny. You can do whatever you want." You are probably tired yourself and so this would be the easiest way to deal with the situation, and certainly the most popular. On the other hand, you could say, "Absolutely not, Johnny. Are you out of your mind? You know better than that. Go to your room right now and do your homework." If you do this, you will point Johnny down the path you think he should walk. No doubt Johnny will develop some vague sense that there is a certain way things should be done. He may even do things this way for the rest of his schooling career, but he may never really know why—other than because you said so. But sooner or later, two roads are going to diverge in the yellow wood of Johnny's life and you're not going to be there to point him down one or the other. Sooner or later Johnny is going to have to make his own decisions.

If all you do is say yes or no, and bark out instructions to be followed in some parrotlike fashion, Johnny doesn't really learn how to make decisions. And one of the best things that you can do for your children is to teach them how to make good decisions. Why? Because life is decisions. We are constantly choosing. Every day is just a series of decisions.

Our decisions create habits. Our habits create character. Our character is our destiny. Asking the right questions is a great way to help children develop their decision-making skills.

So, Johnny comes home from school and says, "Mom, can I watch television before I do my homework?" You could ask, "Johnny, do you think that's a good idea?" Now, rather than just talking at him, you've engaged him. Now he is thinking rather than simply reacting, and when we're thinking we are developing, morally, ethically, and spiritually. If you say to Johnny, "No, you cannot watch television," he gets some vague idea about what he should and should not do, but morally, ethically, spiritually he is not developing. Worse than that, he is becoming artificially reliant on you to make decisions for him. Eventually you will not be there to guide him in these things and you have done nothing to prepare him for that moment.

Alternatively, you could say to him, "Johnny, do you think it's a good idea to watch television before you do your homework?" Johnny may say, "Sure, Mom, it's a great idea!" You then ask, "Why is it a great idea?" Again, you have engaged him. He has to think about the course of action he is proposing. He's going further, he's going deeper. Through these simple questions you are making him consider the way he makes decisions. The simple process of asking a few questions is causing him to develop morally, ethically, and spiritually. Johnny then says "Well, Mom, I've been at school all day and I'm exhausted from sitting in class. I need to relax before I do my homework." Fantastic. On most days it is still probably the wrong answer, but he is thinking in ways that are reasonable and logical.

Take Johnny another step further by asking, "Johnny, if you sit down and start to watch television or play your video games, eventually you are going to have to get up, drag yourself away from the television, and do your homework. How hard is it going to be to drag yourself away when the time comes?"

Does this approach take more energy? Does it take more time? It depends how you look at it. I think if you take the time to help your child develop his moral, ethical, spiritual sense today, it will save you a lot of time and energy in the future. But there is no question that it is going to take more time and energy today.

With this approach, little by little, you are not only leading Johnny to discover the right path, but you are teaching him how and why to choose it. You're not just pointing him along the path of right action; you're teaching him the mental processes that empower him to choose the path of right action when you are not around. You are forever empowering him to make healthy choices in his own life.

Great teachers ask a lot of questions. They do it intentionally and patiently. Not because they don't know the answer. But because asking questions is simply the best way to engage people of any age, and we don't truly absorb or learn anything until we are engaged. The best way to teach your children is to ask the right questions.

Let's consider another example.

Mary is your sixteen-year-old daughter. She comes home from school and says, "Dad, can I go to a party on Saturday night?" Now, there are a few ways you can deal with that request. You can say, "Sure, Mary, do whatever you want."

Again, this is the easiest way to deal with the situation. Or you could say, "No, Mary, you cannot go to a party on Saturday night, and your mother and I have decided that we're going to lock you in your bedroom until you're thirty-five." Alternatively, you could ask, "Why do you want to go to this party on Saturday night?" Mary explains, "Well, you know Michael, that really gorgeous guy I've been trying to get to notice me for the last six months? He asked me to go to the party." It seems reasonable, but you ask, "Where's the party at?" Mary replies nonspecifically with, "Down the street." Now you ask, "How will going to the party help you to become a-better-version-of-yourself?" or "Mary, what sort of things do you think might be going on at the party that your mother and I would prefer you not be exposed to?" Let's face it, it is virtually impossible to find a group of sixteen-year-olds gathering for a party today where sex, drugs, and alcohol are not involved in some way. Mary doesn't quite know what to say. She stutters and fumbles around a bit, but the main thing is Mary now knows that you know. So you know, Mary knows, and Mary knows that you know that there are going to be things happening at that party that are not going to help her become the-best-version-of-herself.

It's important to keep the vision before you at all times, and before them. They need to know that you are not arguing against the party, you are arguing for the-best-version-of-themselves.

You ask Mary, "Do you think it's really a good idea to expose yourself to those sorts of things?" Mary may agree, but more likely she will disagree. Even if she does agree internally, she will very likely still put up a fight. That's what teenagers do. Either way, little by little, you're engaging Mary. You're getting her to think. You are developing her moral, ethical, and spiritual senses. You are presenting a vision for her and her life—to become the-best-version-of-herself—and you are giving her a practical education in how to make her choices with that vision in mind. She's learning how to make good choices; she's learning how to make decisions that help her to live a life brimming with love, happiness, and success.

Eventually, you may have to sit her down and say "Listen, Mary, your mother and I have decided that you can't go to that party on Saturday night for these reasons. . . . But if you really want to spend some time with Michael, invite him here to the house Saturday night, you can have dinner with us. After dinner, the two of you can watch a movie or just sit around and talk in the living room, we'll give you some privacy. But your mother and I just don't think it's a good idea for you to be exposed to what might go on at that party on Saturday night." You can explain to her that if Michael really wants to be with her, he will come, and that if he doesn't come that says something about who he is. Here is another opportunity to talk to her about what she should be looking for in a man.

Through all of this you gain the respect of your sixteen-year-old daughter. She may not like it and is unlikely to admit that you are right for another ten years, but she understands. You are not just an unjust dictator of a parent, you are a loving parent who cares deeply about the welfare of your child. You are a parent with a vision and the courage to lead in the direction of that vision. Has all this worn you out? Probably. Would it have been easier to just say yes? Absolutely. But you would have been making a poor investment in your child's future. Morally, ethically, and spiritually, you've taken the time to engage her, and you've challenged her to think, to grow, to develop, all by asking the right questions.

In this age of advanced technological communications, simply sitting down and taking the time to ask a few questions remains one of the most powerful ways to communicate and educate our young people. The questions we ask of life determine the answers we get and the path we walk.

In my own journey, there is one question that towers above all others. In fact, in many ways this one question has defined my journey. I call it the big question. As far as I am concerned, in our quest to give our lives direction, it is the only question. It is this: God, what do you think I should do? I ask it when small decisions lay before me. I ask it in my time for prayer and reflection each day about the larger questions that loom before me. Sometimes it takes different forms. Consider this question as an example: Which of the options before me will help me to become a-better-version-of-myself? This question is simply a derivative of the big question (God, what do you think I should do?) because I believe that God wants me to become the-best-version-of-myself. But more than that, and beyond that, I believe God has created me (and you) to do some definite service. God has committed some work to me in this moment of history that he has not committed to anybody else. There is a mission uniquely designed for me. My talents, abilities, personality, and all the opportunities that collide with my life all come together to make me the ideal candidate for that mission. If I turn my back on my mission, my actions will echo throughout all of history until the end of time and into eternity.

Interestingly enough, but certainly not surprising upon reflection, the happiest times in my life have been those when I have earnestly asked the big question, patiently waited upon the answer, and perseveringly sought to live out the answer I received in quiet reflection. To be sure, there have been no shortage of times when I have ignored the question out of selfishness, laziness, ego, pride, or any number of defects in my character. These times have been the great low points in my life, even though they have at times been accompanied by my greatest worldly successes.

Perhaps you have not asked the big question in quite a while. It is completely possible that you have never asked it. If that is the case, this is a great moment of grace and I beg you to earnestly consider the question in the days and weeks ahead. And if you ask the question, you may be wondering what you can expect to hear in reply. If you are married and a parent, then your primary vocation concerns your spouse and your child (or children). Your work may be important, it may be powerful and praised, but it is secondary. Your marriage and family are primary. You may be wondering why this is so. The reason is because your marriage and family provide the best opportunity in your life for you to grow in virtue and character, and thus become with every passing day a-better-version-of-yourself. So, if you have the courage to ask the question and the patience to wait quietly on the answer, you will likely find that you are called to dedicate yourself to becoming your best self and to love your spouse and children in a way that helps them to do the same.

You are making decisions every single day of your life—as a person, as a spouse, as a parent, as an employee, and as a citizen. Some of them are small and some of them could alter the whole direction of your life and relationships. When was the last time you sat down in the classroom of silence with the Divine Architect and said, "Show me the plan." When was the last time you sat down with the Divine Navigator and said, "Give me some direction." When was the last time you stepped into the classroom of silence, and sat with your God, and said, "God, what do you think I should do?" This is the question that should dominate your inner dialogue. It's the big question, the ultimate question. And if this is not the question that is dominating your inner dialogue, what question is? What's in it for me? What will bring me the most pleasure? What is the least I can do? What will people think of me?

What question do your children think dominates your inner dialogue? How do they think you make your decisions? Do they think you make your decisions based on personal preferences? Do they think you pray about your decisions? Because if they think you're making all the decisions based upon your mood or preferences on any given day, sooner or later they're going to think that they can make their decisions the same way. If they think you're making the decisions on your own, then subconsciously they attribute to you the rightful place of God. And sooner or later they are going to start attributing to themselves the place of God in their lives. But if they see you turning to God as your guide and counsel in times of decision-making, they will learn to do the same. Probably not here and now, today, but somewhere in the future when they are not so young and sure of themselves, when life throws them a curveball and they don't know what to do, they will turn to the great Guide and Counselor of our lives and find comfort and answers to the questions of their lives.

Words are powerful and significant. They speak of motive and intention, and they communicate much more than we often realize. One simple example of this is when we say to our children, "Let me think about it." It's mundane. It's everyday. And perhaps think about it is all we do. But if we say to them, "Let me pray about it," we communicate something altogether different. If we do then in fact pray about it, it is also likely that we will deliver to them an altogether different answer than if we simply thought about it.

Asking the right questions is powerful in our lives as individuals, spouses, and parents. In fact, in many ways we have betrayed young people by asking them the wrong question as a culture, and in doing so failed to introduce them to the big question. Consider for a moment the most common question we ask children. When they are small we ask them: What do you want to be when you grow up? They tell us they want to be firemen or nurses, teachers or lawyers. When they are in high school we ask them: What do you want to major in when you go to college? They tell us they want to study business, engineering, political science, communications, or perhaps they are undecided. When they are in college we ask them: What do you want to do when you graduate? They tell us they want to get a job in a big city and live the life of a young single professional before they have to take on all the responsibilities of being a full-fledged, contributing, adult member of society. So, when they graduate college they go off and do exactly what they want to do. Does it make them happy? No. They slowly march amid Thoreau's masses leading lives of quiet desperation, and with every passing day they become more and more like those very masses they never imagined they would be like. Now they are confused and disoriented. They followed the path we put before them. The problem is we led them down the wrong path. How did we do it? By asking the wrong question.

What do you want to do? This is the wrong question. I've asked, answered, and followed this question many times in my life, but it never led me to happiness. It led me to self-importance, pride, lust, greed, envy, deceit, and heartache. But never to the joy of a-better-version-of-myself, or a clear conscience, or the peace that comes from knowing that who I am and where I am and what I am doing makes sense.

The happiest people I know are not the people who do whatever they want. In fact, I know plenty of people who because of fame, fortune, position, and power can in fact do whatever they want, whenever they want, and most of them number among the unhappiest people I know. No, such liberty is not the recipe for happiness. The happiest people I know are the ones who have asked and answered the big question, and are seeking to live the answer they were given. The happiest people I know are those who have a sense of mission in their lives, and you don't choose a mission; you are called to a mission.

You may then be wondering what is the right question to

ask young people. There are many variations of the big question that apply. What do you feel called to? How do you feel you could use your talents, abilities, and personality to best serve society? What do you think your mission is in this life? What is God saying to you about your future?

The first time you ask these questions you may get some blank stares, but simply asking the question makes them aware of a different approach. Simply by asking the question, you make them start thinking, consciously or unconsciously, about the answer. It may be ten, twenty, even thirty years before they start to take such questions really seriously, but it is never too early to plant the seed in their hearts and minds.

Questions are powerful. The right question can change the direction of a conversation, a relationship, a life, a business, a church, a nation, even the entire human family. Ask the right questions of yourself, of your spouse, of your children. If you ask the wrong question you will always get the wrong answer. As an individual, a spouse, or a parent, one of the most important skills you can develop is to ask the right questions—both of yourself and of others. Life is as much about the questions you ask as it is about the answers you find.

We All Need an Obsession

One of the many privileges my work has afforded me is the opportunities I have to work with young people, particularly teenagers. Over the past decade I have worked with more than half a million high school students, and people are always asking me questions about them. But the question I have been asking myself for years now is: What do they all have in common? The answer of course is many things, and most people can probably name most of the things these young people have in common. The surprise discovery for me has been their need for an obsession.

As I have reflected on it, I have come to believe we all need an obsession, not just young people. We need it because paradoxically a healthy obsession brings focus and balance to our minds and lives. In addition, obsessions breed passion, energy, enthusiasm, and vitality. It is obsession that gets us out of bed in the morning, and those of us who don't have one find it just that little bit harder to get out of bed with each passing year. What is your obsession? Do you have one?

Of course, it is important to note that obsessions can be good or bad. How do we know which are good and which are bad? Easy enough, those that help us to become a-better-version-of-ourselves are the ones we should pursue and cele-brate.

So, when I visit high schools, it helps me to think of the students as young men and women in search of an obsession. As a parent, I think it could be useful to be aware that they are naturally searching for something, someone, or some-where to obsess about.

Unfortunately, more and more young people are latching on to negative obsessions earlier in life. These obsessions are self-destructive, and rather than breathing passion, energy, enthusiasm, and vitality into their young lives, they often fan a flame of disillusionment and depression. Traditionally, these self-destructive obsessions have been sex, drugs, and alcohol. And while these are playing an ever-increasing role in the lives of teenagers today, there are other obsessions taking central positions in the youth culture that are much more subtle and insidious. This new breed include obsession with body image, having all the right possessions, and the exploration of the Internet.

Have young people always had obsessions? Absolutely. Most of us pass through several, if not dozens, in the course of our youth. My own were cricket, soccer, piano, golf, and business. I'm sure interwoven with these were dozens of fad obsessions, but I grew out of them. I still enjoy these things, but I am not obsessed with them. The disturbing reality about the obsessions in which our young people are getting caught up today is that they tend to have highly addictive qualities and a long-lasting psychological impact. Designer drugs, sexual encounters in their early teens, Internet porn, or the overwhelming violence of video games, take your pick. This is just a sampling of the smorgasbord of self-destructive and addictive behaviors that your children are being presented with each and every single day of their young lives. And if you think your children are not being exposed to these things, then you desperately need to wake up. It is everywhere, and I mean *everywhere*. In places where you would least expect it, it is often more rampant and available than anywhere else.

The types of obsessions that we need are the positive ones that allow us to discover our abilities and boundaries. Those that challenge us and draw us out of our shells, teaching us confidence and the very joy of being passionate about something. We were created to be passionate about something, to obsess over something. This is another reason why young people fall in love so easily and so deeply. Not just a little crush, but all-consuming obsessive love. They yearn for it because they were created for it. This of course can be healthy or unhealthy, but it is mostly the latter because it is misplaced. This is what most of us do with our obsession—we misplace it. We obsess over possessions, acceptance, careers, relationships, and all manner of passing things, instead of finding a lasting obsession to focus upon.

We have this capacity for obsession for a reason, and yet when we place it on things that are temporary, we always seem to end up feeling dissatisfied. The reason is because we are supposed to focus our obsession on a quest more meaningful and lasting, the quest to become the-best-version-of-ourselves. Each and every day of our lives this quest provides exciting challenges and opportunities. This is where the focus of our obsession belongs. The Christian saints strived to become the-best-version-of-themselves because they believed it was the best way to love God and neighbor with their whole hearts, minds, bodies, and souls. Other men and women have dedicated themselves to the quest for many reasons and varied motives. Some of these motives are better than others, but that is another discussion. What's important to understand here is that we all need an obsession. Obsession animates us and brings meaning to our daily lives. Obsession makes the trials tolerable and triumphs meaningful. Your children are going to obsess over things, people, places, and activities. Some will be lasting and others will fade. Some will be a positive influence, others a negative influence. Some obsessions are outright destructive and I pray that as a parent you never have to stand by and see your child suffer at the hands of such an obsession. The point is this: your children are searching for an obsession to give their lives to. Simply being aware of that will make you a better parent.

The Role of Education

My father grew up in poverty in London. He was poor in ways that I cannot begin to imagine, and by hard work, strength of will, and some grace, he made his way in this world. Though he never said it, he worked hard to give my seven brothers and me a better life than his own. It made him happy and proud to see us enjoying opportunities and privileges that were nothing more than pure fantasy to him as a child. Like so many of his generation, he placed a premium on education, but even more so than his peers since my father received no formal education beyond the age of twelve. If he was going to give us nothing else, he was dedicated to giving us a first-rate education.

Mildred Othmer believed education was the answer to many of the problems in our world. In 1998, Mildred died in her Brooklyn home where she had lived for decades. Three years earlier her husband, Donald, had died. Both Mildred and her husband were dedicated to education; he as a college professor and she as a schoolteacher. The Othmers were described by friends and neighbors as having lived comfortably and modestly. You can imagine everyone's surprise when they learned that Donald and Mildred left behind assets of more than $800 million, all of which was left to charity, mostly to colleges and universities.

There are hundreds of stories across the country and around the world that support the esteem in which we hold education. For decades we have seen it as the answer to so many of our problems as individuals, communities, and nations. And while I will concede my own great esteem for education, I think it is important, particularly as parents, that we consider how educating our children fits into our vision for raising amazing children.

Let us then consider the story of Art Katz. He, too, dedicated himself to education. One of the great minds of his times, he believed that the world needed to be educated so that atrocities like those of the Holocaust would never again take place in the world. He believed that education was the answer. After many years of education himself, and many more of teaching, he finally summoned the courage to visit the place where so many of his ancestors were shamelessly put to death.

Standing in one of the concentration camps on a cold winter's afternoon he was overcome by the most startling and disarming discovery of his life. It occurred to him that the Holocaust was not the result of lack of education. He realized that the German people of the 1930s and 1940s were not uneducated. This was no uncivilized tribe, but a highly educated, civilized nation. This was a people who had given rise to the thought leaders in many fields, including Einstein. This discovery perplexed him.

As he drove that afternoon, it began to rain and his car broke down at the side of the road. He walked for quite some time before he came to a small house where he knocked looking for help. The man in the home welcomed him and proceeded to tend to his every need. Together they attended to the car, Mr. Katz bathed and dried himself in the stranger's home, and they dined together. When it was finally time to be on his way, perplexed by the goodness and generosity of his host, he asked, "Why have you been so good to me this day?" The elderly gentleman replied, "My Christian faith demands that I love my neighbor by serving him in need." Years later, Katz explained that at that very moment he became Christian, realizing that love not education was the answer to the world's many dilemmas. Not a theory of love, or words about love, but a real, practical, and daily demonstration of love for one another.

I share all this, because I think it is of paramount importance that parents consider everything in the context of their vision for their children. Education is a wonderful and powerful opportunity for any young person, but our decisions about education cannot be made in a vacuum. Education, along with everything else, should be considered before the backdrop of our larger, broader vision, which is for our children to grow wise enough, strong enough and free enough to choose and celebrate the-best-version-of-themselves in whatever circumstances are presented by daily life.

Education is not intrinsically good. The Nazis taught their officers how to exterminate six million Jews. Gangs in most major cities teach their young members how to deal, steal, and kill. I think we can agree that not all education is good education. The lessons we learn are what determine the quality of an education.

And so, it is perhaps time for us to reconsider what exactly constitutes a good education. This is something we should consider not only as parents in the narrow context of where to send our children to school, but also as members of society where the fruits of our educational choices are harvested daily. The parade of executives charged in recent years for dishonest and deceitful dealings had supposedly been the recipients of the best education money could buy. Horrific crimes of violence are committed daily by highly educated people. But in every case, what is missing is character.

In recent years an enormous movement known as Character Education has sprung up across the United States and beyond. But doesn't it tell us something that such a movement is even required? And is it enough to have a couple of guest speakers visit from time to time to discuss the importance of character in our lives? This approach only makes character appear as an optional extra on the smorgasbord of life, and if the education system approaches it in that way, how can we honestly expect our children to do otherwise? Character education should be at the very heart of our curriculum.

The word *education* comes from the Latin verb *educare,* which means to draw out. Education at its best focuses on drawing out the-best-version-of-each-student. Unfortunately, in our push for more and more money and things, our education system has become more and more focused on imposing upon. We impose upon the students this, that, and the other . . . and then they are ready for corporate America. Is it any wonder so many people are so miserable in their jobs. Did they ever really have a chance to consider what contribution they are here to make?

I think one of the hardest decisions a parent has to make today surrounds the question of where to send their children to school. Sadly, many have no choice. But when we are assessing what makes a good education and where to educate our children, I don't think the question is which school has the best graduation rate, the highest GPAs, or the highest percentage of students accepted to certain colleges. No. We should be looking for character and leadership. Do the teachers have character? Is the principal tough but fair? Is there a vision at work or are we simply trying to meet some standardized testing requirements and get everyone on the bus?

Education is powerful and important: far too powerful and important to be administered without a vision. And our vision of no child left behind is far too small, in far too many ways. It is time to start educating toward character again. Character education should not be an adjunct program in our schools, public or private; it should be the very heart and soul of the core curriculum. We have harnessed the power of science and technology, made tremendous advances in fields that our parents never even considered. Now the question is: Do we have the character to direct our discoveries in ways that genuinely make the world a better place for our children to live in and enjoy? Our culture is teetering on the edge between an age of peace and abundance and an age of unimagined turmoil and heartache—and it is our character that will determine which way the balance shifts.

There has never been a more important time to arm the great minds of our time with character unmatched in any age.

Work and Rest

One of the most powerful ways parents influence their children is with their attitudes toward work and rest. My father never slept in a day in his life. The only time he was ever in bed after seven a.m. was toward the end of his life when his battle with cancer was getting the best of him and he was simply not able to get out of bed. Other than that, I don't have a single memory of my father sleeping in, ever. From where I stand, I see that as both a good thing and a bad thing. Good because it was mostly driven by his gratitude for life and his attitude that each day should be grasped and lived to the fullest. I see it as a bad thing because I think, in some ways, because of his childhood, he was simply unable to allow himself the luxury of sleeping in. Sometimes in my teenage years when I would sleep in, he would come by my room in the morning and ask me if I needed to get up. Or at night he would ask my brothers and me if we needed him to wake us in the morning. He always seemed perplexed when I explained that I didn't need to get up at any particular time, or that I would just get up when I woke up. This was completely foreign to him. But even today, when I sleep in, I tend to feel a little guilty. It isn't that I think my father would think less or me, it's just a habit of the mind that I have found hard to shake. My father didn't want to make me feel guilty about sleeping in for the rest of my life, he was simply living life the way he knew how. The attitudes and behaviors of our parents have enormous influence on us.

I have had many conversations about this with my good

friend Tony, who is one of thirteen children. His father was constantly on their case about keeping busy. Like many of his generation, Tony's father believed that idleness was the devil's playground. He may have been right, but his extreme approach has scarred his children forever. Tony freely admits that he has trouble just sitting down and relaxing. He feels as if he needs to constantly be doing something. Intellectually, he knows the importance of slowing down and taking it easy from time to time, but he struggles to do it. As a child, whenever his father saw him and his siblings sitting around doing nothing, he would yell at them and give them some chore. Sometimes he would have them dig ditches in the yard just to give them something to do. And so, even today, from beyond the grave, his father is affecting his daily life. Not surprisingly, today, many of Tony's siblings would freely admit they are workaholics. Fortunately, Tony has come to recognize the situation for what it is, and with the love and support of his wife for several years now, he has been learning the art of being able to do nothing for an afternoon, or a few days while on vacation. But from time to time, he finds himself gripped by his father's parenting spirit and has to tear himself loose from it.

What attitudes are you teaching your children about rest?

There is, of course, no shortage of examples in the other direction: parents who do nothing. Possessed by the spirits of procrastination and laziness, they seem to spend their whole lives resting up. The attitudes we convey to children about rest can powerfully impact their lives forever.

Another powerful area of influence for parents is that of work. People spend most of their lives working. They spend more time at work than they do with their spouses and children. They spend more time working than they do sleeping or eating. They spend more time working than they do exercising, reading, vacationing, or pursuing hobbies and interests. We spend a lot of time working. The average American will spend more than 100,000 hours working during the course of his or her career. Needless to say, the attitudes with which we approach our work are critical to the happiness we experience in life.

Many people may react to the preceding paragraph by concluding that we simply work too much. I am sure there are many people who work too much, but for most of us that is not the real problem. Work is a natural part of our lives and plays a critical role in our quest to become the-best-version-of-ourselves. We don't just work because we need the money. Sadly, this is how we view work in our modern culture, but the deeper and greater purpose of work is that when we work hard and pay attention to the details of our work, we become a-better-version-of-ourselves. When we work hard, we develop virtue. Hard work breeds patience, fortitude, self-possession, and any number of other virtues.

My own father enjoyed his work. Sometimes he came home a little stressed, but it was only occasionally. Nine out of ten days he came home having had a good day at work. I like working myself and I have no doubt that my father's attitude toward work formed that in me from an early age.

On the other hand, there are many people whose parents didn't enjoy their work. If my father had come home every night complaining about his job and belittling his boss, I suspect I would have a very different attitude toward work. I also don't think it is any coincidence that I have found something to do with the professional aspect of my life that I really enjoy doing. From an early age, I saw that it was possible to do something that you love doing. My father sold industrial catering equipment. A couple of times I asked him why he liked doing it so much. To be honest, I never saw the appeal. I could never understand his passion for it. He told me, "Matthew, I love business. I love selling my products. But it is not about the products; it is about the people. What I love about my job is the relationships I've formed. I love visiting my customers at their bakeries. I love that some of them have been my customers for forty years. I love watching their businesses and families grow. I love people, Matthew, and that's why I'm good at business, because business is about people." For my father, he could have been selling any good product. It was the relationships that he was passionate about. There were parts of his work that he didn't enjoy too much, the paperwork and the budgeting, but he knew these were necessary to have the part of his work that got him out of bed excited for each day.

My mother also had a wonderful attitude toward work. Though she never worked outside the home during my lifetime, she would tell stories about the jobs she had had as a young woman, which also contributed to the positive feelings I had when I entered the world of work as an adult.

We all have good days and bad days at work, and I don't think we should mask that from our children. But regardless, when we come home from work we should be aware that how we reflect on our day at work (through our words and actions) is influencing the way our children will view and approach work forever.

In the same way, if you are really unhappy in your work, one of the best things you can do for your children is to find a job that you can be passionate about. Seeing you passionate and engaged in your work shows them that it is possible to have a job that is challenging and satisfying.

Beyond our attitude toward work itself, parents also consciously and unconsciously exude enormous influence on the actual work their children end up doing. Some parents drive their children toward certain professions by the way they behave, others drive their children away from certain professions by trying to coax their children into them.

In this regard, I am most surprised by the attitudes of the wealthy. I see parents who have enough money to live fifty lifetimes lavishly driving their children toward careers they consider financially lucrative. I can understand this attitude among the urban poor and the middle class, but I am perplexed by it among the wealthy. Surely these parents are in a position, more than most, to encourage their children to do something they are passionate about, or better yet, to pursue a career in which they can best make a contribution to society. Instead, they herd their children toward sixty-hour weeks in accounting firms and law practices.

But regardless of our financial position and means, as parents we should be encouraging our children to explore their unique talents and abilities, pursue some professional vocation that they can approach passionately, and explore what contribution they can make to society with the professional aspect of their lives.

If you knew you would never have to worry about money, that you would always have enough for all you need and most of what you wanted, what work would you dedicate yourself to? My work in the corporate world as a consultant has taught me that most people would not be doing what they are doing. This doesn't mean that they are all miserable in what they are doing, simply that they would rather be doing something else. And most of the time the reason they give is because they feel they could make more of a contribution doing something else. One of the greatest daily tragedies of the modern age is the enormous mismatch that exists between what people do and what they are really good at doing. Let's help our children find their way in this world to a career that allows them to pay their bills, enjoy the things of this world, and at the same time be passionate about their work and experience the satisfaction of making a difference.

My father didn't rest enough, and when I am completely honest with myself, I know I work too hard and too much. But my father loved his work and I believe his love for his work was contagious and I caught it. I'm glad I did. Going to work each day to a job that I love, in my belief, is one of life's great privileges. I'm trying to work a little less, and I'm trying to allow myself to relax a little more without feeling guilty about it. I'm a work in progress, but mostly I am enjoying the adventure.

A Philosophy About Money

In this day and age, we give young people education opportunities beyond compare, and yet one of the areas we teach them virtually nothing about is money. What we do teach them about money is often more of a liability than an asset. Your children will need money knowledge simply to survive in the money world. If they are going to thrive, our children need a higher level of money knowledge than any generation before, and yet, we send them out into the world often without even the basics, like sheep to the slaughterhouse.

It has been my experience that when it comes to money, there are only two types of people: savers and spenders. At one end of the spectrum, the extreme savers hoard as much of their income as they can. They find it difficult to enjoy buying things they really want. Often they even feel guilty about buying things they need. At the other end of the spectrum, the spenders let money slip through their hands like water. They seem simply incapable of resisting the impulse to buy. All their purchases seem necessary and they often cannot understand why they never have any money.

These are, of course, extreme examples, and there are people at various intervals along the spectrum, but it is amazing how extreme most of us are when it comes to money. The irony is that savers tend to attract spenders in relationships.

Money is an opportunity to teach our children so many valuable lessons about self and life. I would love to write a whole book for you on this topic alone, but let's focus here on just a handful of the basics.

Last year, I was visiting my friends Pat and Laura in the San Francisco Bay area. They have three wonderful children, and when I arrived at their home, the boys were just getting ready for bed. Their father was reading them a story, and their mother suggested the boys would like me to say hello.

So I went into the bedroom where the boys were gathered around their father. Looking around the room, I noticed that the two oldest boys, Connor and Matthew (whose room we were all in), each had three glass jars on their dressers. Each jar had a handwritten label stuck on it. The first read SAVINGS, the second read SPENDING, and the third CHARITY.

After Pat had finished reading them the book, he kissed the boys good night, got them into bed, and turned out the lights. Later that evening when we were out at dinner I asked him about the jars. I was intrigued by them. He explained that when the boys are given money, either for doing a chore or in a birthday card from their grandma, they divide it between the three jars. Ten percent for charity, 10 percent for savings, and the rest for spending. What a powerful way to educate children about money. It is so disarmingly simple, but consider the lessons.

First and foremost, these boys are forming powerful habits. Any person who saves 10 percent of his or her income is sure to live in relative financial security and independence sooner or later. The average American saves less than 1 percent of his or her income (outside of retirement contributions). Children are never too young to learn the habit of saving.

They are also forming the powerful habit (and virtue) of generosity. By allocating 10 percent of their income to charity, they are learning to give to those in need and to causes they believe in. This lesson makes them aware that there are a lot of organizations out there doing good things for people in need. At the end of each quarter, they decide which charity or charities to give their money to. This provides another powerful lesson: that you cannot give to them all.

These are important lessons, but this exercise also teaches them to enjoy spending. In my own life I have always found it difficult to spend money on myself. I can buy things for other people without batting an eyelash, but I struggle to buy things that I really want for myself. I am more inclined to deny myself and save that money. In recent years, I have started doing something similar to what the boys do. Namely, allocating a certain percentage of my income to spend. I can spend it on whatever I want as long as I don't go over the allocated amount. This has freed me from the guilt that has often prevented me from enjoying the money I have earned. The boys' third jar is marked spending. They can spend their money on whatever they want, and in so doing, learn the valuable lesson that life is about the allocation of scarce resources.

From time to time, Pat and Laura tell me that one of the boys will want to buy something that they don't have enough money in their spending jar to buy. They will plead for permission to take or borrow from their savings jar or their charity jar. The easy thing for Pat and Laura to do would be to give them the extra money or to let them borrow or take the money from the other jars. But they don't, because the lesson would be lost. This is how most people live their lives financially. They simply lack the discipline to create a plan and stick to it. They simply lack the discipline required to put the money in the jars that they belong in and use it accordingly.

Beyond teaching our children in practical ways how to

manage and use money, our philosophy regarding money and the way we use it can have an enormous impact on our children. My inability to buy things for myself free from guilt is something I inherited from my father. It is something deeply ingrained in me, and something I have to work on consciously to overthrow it. My father had no intention of forming me in this way. He was simply living his life in the best way he knew how. It is just another example of how powerfully we are impacted by the way our parents approach life.

Before moving on, I would like to explore and comment briefly on three trends that are emerging in relation to money in our society today. Each of them is the result of social circumstances unique to our place and time, at least unique in scale.

Let us call the first affluenza. Like influenza, it is a disease that spreads very quickly through social contact with those who are infected. Over the past twenty years, the generation we refer to as the baby boomers have amassed an incredible amount of wealth. Driven by the desire to give their children everything they never had when they were young, and lacking the self-possession to do it in any disciplined manner, they have lavished every kind of indulgence on their children. They have done this with no regard for teaching their children about the laws and properties of money and wealth accumulation, and with equal disregard for whether or not their children will be able to sustain the lifestyle to which they have become accustomed. As a result, the parking lot at many high schools looks like a luxury car dealership. It is not uncommon to see teenage girls sporting thousand-dollar designer label handbags at school, and something as simple as the latest iPod or running shoes is considered to be just a part of their God-given right.

This affluenza gives rise to the second trend, which is an overwhelming sense of entitlement among today's teens and young adults. I am amazed, in my work as a corporate consultant, at how much this attitude of entitlement is affecting the modern workplace. We have moved from the idea that "I deserve a pay raise because I did XYZ, which has added value to this company in this way and that" to the idea that "I am entitled to a pay raise simply because I work here and a year has passed." The bottom line is that when we give people things without adequately educating them about the value of such things, we create an attitude of entitlement. This attitude is one of the most debilitating to the human spirit. There is a long history of failed welfare programs in every modern society around the world. These are proof that when you give people something they have not earned and do not simultaneously empower them to help themselves in the future, you take more from them than you give them because you stifle their spirit and create a sense of entitlement. At the other end of the spectrum, trust funds are little more than welfare for the wealthy. Not surprisingly, we often see the same attitude of entitlement among the recipients of such trust funds.

The third trend that is emerging in a powerful way at this time is parents attempting to buy their children's love. This is the result of two scenarios primarily. The first is where parents are working too much and spending too little time with their children, so they try to compensate for that and overcome their guilt by buying their children things. The second is that, with the growing number of divorces, it is very tempting to try to win favor with our children by buying them things. The outcome of both is that children learn to associate gifts with love, and long after the fact, they will go looking for someone who can love them in that way. The classic example is that of a father who is not emotionally centered enough to love his daughter in ways that are healthy and authentic, so he buys her things, lots of things, maybe everything. In time, the daughter grows into a woman, and what sort of man is she attracted to? The man who buys her things. He may lack substance and goodness, but she draws her model of love from how her father loved her. When we use money or things to win the affection of our children, we distort their view of life and love in ways they will struggle with for the rest of their lives.

Is it natural for parents to yearn to give their children good things and experiences? Yes. Should we give our children the good things of this world? To the extent that our financial means allow us, absolutely. I am not suggesting otherwise. But more importantly, we should do it in ways that help and do not hinder them from finding their own way in this world and becoming the-best-version-of-themselves.

Money is a strange thing. It is either your servant or your master, but never your friend. We all have a philosophy about money, whether we are able to articulate it or not, and this philosophy has an enormous impact on our lives. The interesting thing is, you almost never meet someone who has just enough money. Most people think they have too little and others have too much, but very rarely do you have just the right amount. The thing about having too little is that you are required to live your life in the pursuit of the money you need in order to survive. The thing about having too much is that it becomes harder to live the life you were created for because you are afraid you will lose what you already have. All in all, the thing about money is that it can cause people to do things they don't really want to do just to get their hands on it. Legally and illegally, people do things every day that they simply would not do if they had enough money.

On the other hand, it is easy to dismiss all this talk about money and say that money is not that important. But its importance has grown in our lives over the past hundred years. Our lives have become more complex and more dependent on money than ever before. But the real importance of money stems from the impact it can have on our relationships and its ability to help us or prevent us from living out our dreams and following our destiny.

What is your money philosophy? What philosophy are you passing on to your children—actively and passively— regarding money?

Food, Exercise, and Body Image

Our habits form our futures, and few habits are more powerful than our habits in the areas of food, exercise, and body image. In *The Rhythm of Life* I explained in some detail how our obsession with time management in the twentieth century needed to give way to a mastery of energy management in the twenty-first century. Time management is important and critical to success, but energy management is the next evolution in our quest for excellence. Food and exercise provide two of the three main sources of our physical energy (sleep being the third). Children seem to be filled with boundless energy, but we rarely think to educate them about managing their energy. The problem is, by the time they need to know about energy management, they have often formed a plethora of counterproductive habits in this area . . . and you are no longer around to guide them. Some parents may argue, "They are too young to know about this stuff," or "They wouldn't listen anyway." Keep this in mind: young people are smarter than we give them credit for. They are capable of comprehending things that we consider way beyond them if these things are communicated in the context of a loving, mentoring relationship. They are listening even when they are pretending not to listen. Sixty percent of the stuff they pretend not to be hearing they pass on to their friends within twenty-four hours. And they will be thinking about the things they pretended not to be listening to long after you are dead and gone. Parents only get so much time with their children to educate them about life. It is the most demanding job in the world. Focus on the fundamentals.

Communicating with children is difficult. Communicating with adolescents, I mean really getting inside their hearts and minds, can be almost impossible. So, what is a parent to do? I think we have clearly established that it takes time. You cannot expect to sit down with your children for a couple of minutes each day and have them download all that is happening to them, never mind all that is going on inside their hearts and minds. But after making the time to have a conversation with our children, the next set of factors we need to consider are environment and circumstances.

My parents were wonderful, but they were not perfect. One of the worst things they did was ritually sit down to watch television each night after dinner was finished and everything was cleaned up. Some nights I could see that my mother wanted to talk to my father (or vice versa), but the other was too engrossed in his or her television show or movie. So they would start to talk at the breaks, but the show would return and the conversation would end. It was painful to watch. Even more painful was when, as a teenager, I wanted to talk to them about something, I would come and sit in the living room where they were watching television and wait for the show to end so I could talk to them about whatever it was I wanted to talk to them about. On more than one occasion, I remember picking up the TV listings and seeing that the movie had more than an hour left. I just got up and went to my room.

The circumstances and environments we create to spend time with our children are powerful ways to invite them to communicate with us. Exercise provides a unique opportunity to spend time with them. I am not speaking of watching them at their soccer game or taking them to a baseball game. These are important, but for different reasons. I mean actually working out with them, especially as they get into those teen years. One of the most ingenious strokes of parenting I have seen in all my travels was a father who takes his teenage children bicycling on a tandem bike. He peddles at the front and they peddle at the back. It is a time to spend with his children one-on-one without the pressure or intimidation of sitting across from one another. More than that, it is fun and exhilarating. But even more than that, the physical exercise gets the endorphins pumping, and once the endorphins start to go through our system we think in different ways and act in different ways . . . and yes, communicate in different ways. He finds that out on the bike path he can get his children talking about everything and anything. So much so that I think he questions sometimes if he really wanted to know what they have told him. But as a father, he has found that topics his children will never open up about at home or while driving to a ball game are freely spoken about on the back of the tandem bike once those endorphins are pumping.

Perhaps you don't like riding bikes, or maybe you can't afford a tandem bike, or perhaps you just don't have anywhere to keep it. That's not the point. The point is that this idea can be replicated in a thousand ways that are fun and exciting. The idea is also equally accessible by simply taking a long walk together. It's amazing what your children will share with you on a long walk. Don't push it. Don't force it. Start by talking about yourself and what is happening in your life. Let them into your world, allow them to experience your humanity, and they will freely invite you into their world.

This is just one of the connections that can be formed between parents and children with exercise. Beyond enhancing communication opportunities, one of a parent's many responsibilities is to convey the importance of exercise to his or her children. Needless to say, the best way to convey this to your children is to have a regular and healthy approach to exercise yourself. This means that both extremes should be avoided. If you never work out, or rarely work out, there is no use trying to convince your children about the virtue of regular exercise. In the same way, if you are fanatical about working out, your children are likely to consider you to be abnormal and extreme and will again ignore your counsel.

Children, like almost everyone else on the planet, are looking for someone to lead the way, not point the way. Their constant cry is "Don't tell me. Show me!" In the absence of genuine leadership from parents, coaches, older siblings, mentors, and teachers they can become cynical and disengaged.

Another reason why educating our children about exercise is often neglected is because when they are in school, most children tend to be involved in organized sports that provide plenty of recreational exercise. But a significant number of children drop out of organized sports in their teen years when regular exercise can provide a powerful counterresponse to the explosion of hormones that teenagers experience. Once they graduate from high school only a tiny percentage of students pursue organized sports in college. Add to that a college diet and it is easy to see why many college students return from school after their freshman year ten, fifteen, or twenty pounds heavier than they were when they left.

This of course leads us to the area of diet. How do you eat? How do your children eat? What do you tell your children about food? What does how you eat tell your children about food?

More than 51 percent of children and teenagers are medically considered overweight. One third of those are considered to be obese. The affects of this problem reach into every corner of our lives and our society. On a personal level, obesity affects a person's energy levels, ability to focus, and almost inevitably leads to self-esteem issues. As a society, it affects our efficiency and effectiveness in every arena, diminishes the overall physical health of a nation, and leads to rising health care cost and issues.

Is it a parent's fault that a child is overweight? Not an easy question to answer. In general, the answer is no. Obesity is caused by a number of factors including genetics, diet, exercise, and a person's inability to moderate his or her food intake. At the same time, if we rephrase the question: Can it be a parent's fault that a child is overweight? The answer is, absolutely. At some point, we have to consider that part of the problem here is irresponsible parenting. No aspect of life is free from the reckless behavior of those in positions of influence and authority, and sometimes parents are part of that problem.

In the midst of a culture that is dominated by instant gratification, it is difficult to teach children to discipline themselves when it comes to what they eat. Indeed, it is perhaps equally difficult to approach food in a disciplined manner ourselves. They say an alcoholic can hear the beers in the refrigerator talking to him. In the same way, some people can hear certain types of foods talking to them, calling out to them from the fridge, the pantry, their desk drawer, the store down the street. Resisting our cravings can seem almost impossible at times.

The key to success in just about everything we have discussed in this book is keeping sight of the vision: to become the-best-version-of-ourselves. Is what you are about to eat going to help you become a-better-version-of-yourself?

The reason why it is so important to keep this vision in sight is because it is impossible to say no to anything unless you have a deeper yes. You say no to a burger and have a salad instead by reminding yourself of your deeper yes for health and well-being. You work out instead of watching television for hours because you have a deeper yes for health and well-being and the increased energy it brings you.

I am not going to give you a list of do's and don'ts. Most of them only work as long as you hold to a vision. Some people's vision is to lose ten pounds. They stick to a diet or regimen until they do and then they fall back into their old habits. I am giving you a vision not for a week or a month, or even a year, but a vision for a lifetime.

Don't diet. Learn to eat well. Listen to your body. Is it craving something because it needs it? Or are you craving a certain food as an emotional comfort? Deal with the emotion or the situation that causes the emotion and the craving will go away. Similarly, start to pay attention to when your stomach is full. Know when enough is enough, and stop eating. If you put a bowl of food in front of a dog, how much does she eat? All of it. Some dogs will eat and eat even to the point of making themselves sick. In the same way, if you put a plate of food in front of most people, how much do they eat? All of it. Most people don't even stop to think or wonder, Am I full yet?

We have heard hundreds of stories about people who were told as children to eat all their food because there were children starving in Africa or China. This is absurd on so many levels, but surely at this time in history we could evolve at least in this one area by beginning to teach children to listen to their bodies.

Again, we return to the idea of asking the right questions. When you eat certain types of foods they make you feel heavy and sleepy, when you eat other foods you feel light and energized. Are you aware of how certain foods make you feel? It doesn't hurt to talk about that with your children. Perhaps you are out and you stop for burgers, fries, and a shake. When you get done you feel bloated and tired. Tell your children you feel that way. Ask them how their food feels in their stomach. This simple question will awaken their senses to consider this after they eat, and in time they will hopefully consider it before they eat. Next time you are out and everyone is ordering burgers and you have a healthy alternative instead and your children ask you why, it might be a good idea not to say because you feel fat or because you are watching your weight, but rather explain that you don't like how it feels in your stomach once you are done or that you feel what you have chosen to eat will give you more energy.

Food is fuel for the body, a premium source of energy. A meal is a great reason to gather people together, but eating is not primarily recreational. We eat to fuel our bodies for life. Food is an essential need and plays a critical role in our development, and in sustaining the health and energy required to live out our destinies. In this area, the extreme of overeating tends to get most of the attention of late, but the other extreme continues to be a growing problem among our children, particularly in the adolescent years.

One of the primary areas of concern for young people, and particularly for young women, is the area of eating. Eating disorders are rampant in both high schools and colleges across the country. Anorexia, bulimia, compulsive overeating, and their related emotional and mental symptoms are reaching epidemic levels among today's youth.

These disorders can be triggered by a hundred different circumstances in a hundred different people, but one thing is certain and that is that our obsession with body image in this day and age is fueling these diseases. This brings us to the third rail of our discussion in this section: body image.

There is a certain psychosis that surrounds the area of body image that I am certain has never before existed in the history of humanity. I recently read a report that found that the fastest growing addiction on college campuses was not an addiction to sex, drugs, alcohol, coffee, or smoking, but an addiction to exercise. In a growing number of cases, students are working out for three, four, and five hours a day.

Our obsession with body image causes people to gravitate toward both extremes, and so in the areas of health and wellness, as with just about every aspect of modern life, we find very few people striking a balance somewhere in the healthy middle. This obsession is fueled by television, the movies, magazines, billboards, advertisements, shopping catalogs, store manikins, and the scantily clad models that roam the catwalk and seem to become thinner and thinner with every passing year. But it is also fueled in ways that may seem subtle to some or may be practiced by others who are completely unaware that they are powerfully impacting the psyche of their children or siblings. Allow me to share a couple of brief examples.

The most common example is a father or brother ogling a woman, and making comments like "She's hot" or observing another woman and saying "She's fat" or "She's got a lot of junk in her trunk." It happens every day, more times than anyone could count. But a teenage daughter hears her father (or brother) talking about women in this way and she is automatically conditioned to assess her own body. Her brother and father are expressing acceptance and rejection based purely on physical appearance, and it is impossible for her not to be affected by that.

Needless to say, mothers and sisters say things about men in the same way that can affect children equally powerfully. And, tragically, many women speak in this way about other women. They don't say "she's hot," but they will comment on appearance, often with great severity. "She has such a pretty face, it's a pity she's so fat," and so forth.

Another example, which I am amazed at how often it happens, is when a father comes to his eldest daughter to vent that his wife (her mother) is not taking care of herself physically. When a father says to his teenage daughter, "Your mom has really put on some weight over the past couple of months, and I don't know how to broach the subject with her . . . ," the daughter often deduces that her father's love and acceptance is not unconditional, and that one of the major conditions is that she take care of herself physically. She is likely not emotionally developed enough to deal with the situation at hand in any other way than to internalize and personalize it. The father gets to vent, but at what cost?

Food, exercise, and body image all play a huge role in the lives of children. Our culture focuses on the shallow and superficial. Children need parents to take the discussion about these things to a deeper level, and to bring perspective to these things by presenting them as part of a comprehensive and cohesive vision of life. Let us begin to speak to children about food, exercise, and body image in the broader context of becoming the-best-version-of-themselves. If we do this, we will return the focus in these areas to feeling physically good rather than psychologically and emotionally adequate and acceptable, or inadequate and unacceptable.

The Sex Culture

Where does one even start when it comes to talking to children about sex these days? It's a tough question, but the tougher question surprisingly enough is, Where does one even start when it comes to talking to children's parents about sex? In a 2002 episode of *Friends,* Monica said to Rachel, "I'm so glad you got drunk and had sex," after Rachel had a baby as result of one sexual encounter with Ross. The show went to air, of course, during family prime-time hours on NBC. Something like this is disturbing on a number of different levels to some people, and to others it is simply funny. The point is that we are living in a sexually centered culture, and young people are being immersed in it at younger and younger ages. They are being thrown around by the waves of the sexually focused culture, and they will spend the rest of their lives trying to make peace with the sexual trauma that a growing number of them are being exposed to.

Here are some statistics. Fifty percent of fourteen-year-old girls are experimenting with oral sex. One in four teenagers becomes infected with a sexually transmitted disease. Fifty percent of new HIV infections in the United States are among people under the age of twenty-five. We could examine each of them carefully, and dozens more, but the reality is actually much more frightening than the statistics.

A letter was recently sent home to parents of a school warning parents to be aware that "oral sex parties" are the new trend in eighth grade. I was recently speaking with a friend who is a priest, and he was explaining that he had become alarmed by the number of children ten and eleven years old who were confessing to him that they were participating in sex parties. He investigated a little to discover that these were all the rage in his area. He inquired as to how they take place and was told that the boys are brought into a room, one at a time, and a girl from his class is waiting there for him.

You could ask, Where are the parents? And it is certainly a valid question, but there are issues far beyond that desperately need addressing in this area. Educators and politicians propose two solutions, handing out condoms and abstinence education. Clearly neither is working.

We are no longer talking about a few teenagers exploring their sexuality in ways that are damaging to themselves and others. The exception has become the rule. Parents every-where live in the delusion that their children are not in-volved, and for the most part, they are absolutely kidding themselves. The reality now is that children nine, ten, and eleven years old are exploring their sexuality in ways that will forever affect their ability to relate in a healthy manner (both emotionally and sexually). This is to say nothing of the physical risks and the psychological damage that a single sex-ual encounter can produce. This is one area where the ever-shifting line of relativism is demonstrating the weakness and error of this philosophy, but we ignore the facts before our very eyes.

They are children and they are fragile. In some ways a fifteen-year-old boy or girl may look like an adult, but you know from the ways they think and act in other areas of their lives that they are still just children in many ways. Different people may disagree about sexual ethics, but surely we can all get together and agree that a twelve-year-old or a ten-year-old is simply not ready to be sexually active. The prob-lem with the relativism that forms so much of our thinking today is that the line keeps shifting farther and farther from all that is good, true, beautiful, and noble.

The bottom line is this: talk to your children about sex. They are confused and scared, and they want and need direction. Everyone else is talking to them about sex. The music they listen to, the TV shows they watch, the movies they see, the magazines they read, and their friends at school are all giving them a message about sex. What is *your* mes-sage to your children about sex?

All Things Technology

We have tolerated a great deal in the name of progress over the past fifty years, and technological advancement is constantly heralded as improving our lives. But is technology improving your child's chances of growing into a healthy contributing member of society? Is the technology that seems so commonplace in the lives of today's young people helping them to become the-best-version-of-themselves?

I was having lunch last week with a father who told me that he Googles his children once every six months to see what is out there in cyberspace about them. He explained that the first time he conducted such a search, at the suggestion of another parent, he was amazed at how many references there were on the Internet to his children. Every time their name appears in a paper for a sporting event, or every time the school announces their participation in a new program it finds its way online. Last time he conducted such a search, he was taken on an adventure that included a trip through several of his high school daughter's friends' MySpace pages. He explained that he was disturbed by what was on the MySpace pages, but he was more disturbed at how these pages link his daughter and her friends to people all over the country of all ages. The pages were filled with text and photos, much of which was inappropriate, and certainly not something most teenagers would want their parents to see. But the assumption is that the parents will never see these things. And as this is the first generation of MySpace, most of these children have not even begun to understand the repercussions of what may appear like harmless fun today. Ten years from now, twenty years from now, when they decide they want to run for a political office at any level, these pages will begin to show up in gossip columns and magazines. At any time in the future, but most likely at the least convenient and most embarrassing moment, the content of these pages will emerge to embarrass these children . . . and worse. When I was in high school, it was something if we found a copy of a teacher's old yearbook. In the future, students will be accessing their teacher's old MySpace pages.

Our children don't know this, they don't realize the implications of what they are involved in. They need their parents to guide and protect them.

This, of course, is only scratching the surface of the problems the Internet presents for parents. Where is the computer in your house? In a spare room? In the living room? In your children's bedrooms? Wherever it is, there, at the touch of a keyboard, your children have access to the best and worst of everything, anywhere in the world.

Is the Internet really helping our children become the-best-version-of-themselves?

Moving on, we discover that in the very near future, it won't matter how well you monitor the time they spend at the computer, because they now have Internet access via their cell phones. The cell phone culture among children and teens is extraordinary. We hand them out with little regard for what we are putting in the hands of our children. I heard a seven-year-old ask his parent for a cell phone for Christmas last year. I was there. In the room. He wasn't joking. He wasn't even reaching. But more disturbing is that his parents didn't seem too surprised. And the way that I know they weren't is that his mother said to him, "Not this year, honey, but maybe next year." At first I thought that perhaps she was simply placating him, but I wasn't sure. So I asked her and she said to me, "He needs to learn how to use technology. The way I see it, the sooner the better. It's the way of the future."

A recent survey indicates that a child with a cell phone is six times more likely to be sexually active than a child without one. You may be wondering what a cell phone has to do with sex. Those conducting the survey explained that more than 90 percent of the time, parents have no idea who their children are talking to on their cell phones. They can take them anywhere and they become their link to the world—the good, the bad, and the ugly.

Then there is the *amount* of time teens are spending on cell phones both talking and texting, and we have not even begun to discuss how that time could be better spent.

So, what is a parent to do? Parents ask me all the time about this one and I always suggest the same thing. But I always begin by asking them why they feel it is important for their children to have cell phones. Convenience and safety seem to be what it comes down to. The truth is the kids probably have them because they want them, and they want them because all their friends have them. But convenience and safety are the reasons parents give to justify it. I suggest to parents to have a couple of family cell phones. When your children need them for convenience (yours not theirs) and safety, they can take one. When they don't need it, you have it. It's a simple solution though difficult to implement. The reality is you pay now or you pay later. If we take the time now to help them grow free and strong with a keen sense of who they are and what life is about, we will be able to enjoy who they have grown to become later. If we don't, we will spend the time later trying to help them to do and discover what they should have done and discovered during their childhood and adolescence.

By now I am sure that some parents are thinking that I have lost all sense of reality, that I need to come into the modern world, or that I am being unreasonable. The truth is, I am only just getting started. Which brings us to video games.

Have you seen a video game that portrays a behavior that you would like your child to emulate in his or her life? I didn't think so. What are we thinking? Do we genuinely think that the rise in violence over the past twenty years has not been influenced by the rise in popularity of violent video games? The idea is as absurd as tobacco lobbyists who still claim that smoking doesn't cause cancer. There may not be a handbook for parenting, but if there was, I am pretty sure it would not say on the first page that the first step to being a great parent is to check your common sense with your coat and hat at the door. I'm sure something good comes to a child who learns how to play and excel at video games, but I cannot imagine that it outweighs the many vices that can be easily acquired through this habit.

Put all these things together and you can begin to see what your children are up against in their quest to become the-best-version-of-themselves.

Then, of course, there is television. The average child between five and sixteen spends more than fifteen hours a week watching television. That's fifteen hours of programming, and we are the ones being programmed. But the shows they are watching are not helping them to become all they can be and celebrate their best selves. To the contrary, television for the most part supports the culture's nonvision for the human person. Driven by advertising and consumption and a blatant disregard for what is right or wrong, or good or bad, most programming appeals to the lowest common denominator. And it will come as no surprise that the lowest common denominator gets lower and lower with every passing year. Some people may say that I am going too far, that sometimes entertainment is just entertainment. I agree with the concept. I agree that everything does not need to be intensely purposeful. But is it too much to ask to produce some entertainment that is both relaxing and helps us to become the-best-version-of-ourselves? I think not. Seriously, when was the last time you got up from watching television and thought to yourself, "I am definitely a-better-version-of-myself for having watched that show!" It might happen from time to time, but it doesn't happen that often.

We need to get serious about helping our children pursue a vision for their lives, rather than allowing them to be abused and consumed by the culture.

Consider the people who appear on your television on any given day of the year. Would you let these people take your child out for the day? Would you let these people babysit your children? Would you invite them into your living room?

Would you let them hang out in your son's or daughter's bedroom? You do. They are in your home. They are a part of your life. They are possibly spending more time raising your children than you are.

Finally, let us consider music. Music is one of the most powerful mediums, perhaps the most powerful, for conveying a message. Music has been a part of the teen lifestyle for generations, but never have they had such constant contact with it. Wherever they go, the little white headphones go with them. Have you ever found yourself humming or singing a song, over and over again throughout the day? Sometimes you don't even like the song, but you can't stop and you can't get it out of your head. You try, but resistance is futile. You are consumed by the song that got trapped in your subconscious somewhere during your life and has been bouncing around in your mind ever since, and now is emerging in a way that you don't understand and cannot control. Music is powerful. It is powerful beyond measure and understanding. The message of music has a conscious and subconscious affect on our lives. So, what is the message of the music that most teens are listening to today? At the soft end of the spectrum it surrounds a very selfish view of love that is mostly limited to the shallow waters of physical attraction and sexual exploration. At the hard end of the spectrum the message is about killing cops, disrespecting woman, explicit references to sex and drugs, getting what's yours, pimps and whores, foul language, and other related topics. Is this a message you would give to your children? Would you take them to a lecture that was going to explain how to commit acts of sex and violence? Would you read them a book that explained how to make it on the streets as a pimp and a drug dealer?

Parenting is not easy. As Erma Bombeck once wrote, "Parenting is not for wimps." It requires real effort and adherence to a vision. So, let me ask you. If your children did not watch television or go to the movies for three months, and if they didn't go on the Internet, use a cell phone, or play video games for three months . . . would they be better-versions-of-themselves? Would you have better relationships with them? Would you communicate more as a family?

We know the answers to these problems, we just don't like the answers. You are at war. What are you willing to sacrifice to win that cultural war? What is at stake? The lives of your children in more ways than one. Are you willing to celebrate and defend the vision? Are you willing to be tough but fair, to really love your children and help them to build a future rich in wisdom and opportunities? These are tough questions, and we have been avoiding them for too long already.

Foster a Spirit of Service

There is a lot of crossover between the skills required to effectively parent and those required to effectively manage people and projects in the workplace. In the corporate environment, great managers are constantly seeking out the best practices and new ideas to help them stay ahead of the curve. This desire for continuous learning and improvement can be found in the leaders of any field, including parenting.

The most effective parents are always looking for new ways to engage their children in their own development. To most young people, life is free of the confusion and complications and responsibilities that come with adulthood, and so it is easier for them to ignore the need to learn and grow. This can result in a complacency that can seriously stunt a person's ability to participate fully in life socially and, later, emotionally. To avoid this, parents can call on one of the great management advances of all times.

For thousands of years the rule for managing people had been management by actions. The manager says "Do this!" and the worker does it. Modern managers realized the ineffective nature of this style and thus was born management by results. In this model the manager explains to the worker what she wants achieved, and the worker is free to use his skills and resources to accomplish that task within the value and standard structure of the organization.

As a parent, you are to a certain extent managing your children. What is your management style? Do you manage by actions? Do this, do that, and so on. Or do you manage by results? Explain a vision, and allow them to use their skills and resources to accomplish it. In the latter case, you are of course part of their resources. If they get stuck or don't know what to do, they can call on you—and good managers clearly communicate that. "I'm here for you if you need me, but I don't want to get in the way."

There are many differences between these two styles, but the greatest difference is this: In the first scenario, management by actions, if the manager is not around, the workers cannot do anything. They are completely disempowered. They lack the courage and the independence to act without the presence of their manager. The workers are dependent on

their manager. In the second scenario, management by results, the workers can be busy about their work whether the
manager is present or not, and continue in this way until they
come upon a situation that exceeds their knowledge, at
which time they call on their manager because they have
been trained to do so.

Management by actions makes the worker dependent on
the manager. Management by results creates independent
workers who can think and act for themselves, and who
know who and where to turn when they don't know how to
handle a situation. Mediocre managers make their workers
dependent and themselves indispensable. Great managers
make their workers independent and themselves dispensable.

As a parent, your job is to make yourself dispensable.

If you parent by actions, sooner or later your children are
going to find themselves in situations where they have to decide for themselves—and they will be handicapped because
you never developed this skill set in them.

It is not enough, as a parent, to match certain behaviors
with certain situations. It is not enough to model these behaviors. Parenting is much more involved than saying yes or
no. It is much more complicated than simply saying you can
or cannot do certain things. At the core of parenting is the
difficult and complex task of nurturing a child's ability to
choose and decide and act for him- or herself. This requires
certain skills in our children, but also that we nurture the
character and values to guide those skills.

There are few ways more powerful to nurture these skills,
values, and character than to foster and encourage a spirit of
service.

We are not here for ourselves. We are not in this alone. We are here, in this place and this time, to experience each other and to act in communion with each other for the good of each other. Yes, we are also here to discover and celebrate our unique selves. But paradoxically, the best way to find and celebrate our true selves is to spend our lives in the service of worthy causes and other people.

Service awakens our sense of self in a way that all the introspection and self-development in the world cannot. Nothing awakens the moral, ethical, and spiritual senses like the simple act of service.

As a child, I can distinctly remember my father coming home from work at night and asking my mother, "Is there anything I can do to help?" My mother was getting dinner ready or helping us with our homework, or both. Usually she said there was nothing. Occasionally she asked my father to do something small to help things run a little more smoothly. Why do I distinctly remember this? Probably because it happened often. Did it happen every day? I'm sure it didn't, but it happened regularly enough that I learned how to act. The reason I know this is because I started coming home from school and asking my mother, "Is there anything I can do to help?" From time to time, my father would reinforce this lesson by saying, "Go and ask your mother if she needs our help with anything." And today, wherever I go, I have an extra sense that alerts me when people around me need assistance with something. Do I always help them? No. But I am aware that they are in need of help. That sense is alive within me.

One of the greatest gifts my parents ever gave me was the spirit of service. It is not passed on by saying do this or do that. It is instilled in others by an example of being available to others in their need. Usually it is just small kindnesses and common courtesy, and yet both have become all too uncommon in our modern culture.

I think if you sat most parents down and asked them, "Do you want your children to grow up to be self-centered?" most parents would say no. But it is not enough to know what you don't want in this world. It is critical that you know the outcome you wish to achieve. So, taking it a step further. If we don't want our children to be self-centered, what is it that we want? The opposite reality of self-centered is others-centered.

To live an others-centered life is certainly something that is countercultural at a time where young people are actively encouraged to go out and get whatever it is they want for themselves from life. Somewhere, somehow, we have been convinced that living an others-centered life is not going to bring happiness to us. Nothing could be further from the truth. The happiest people I know are those who have dedicated themselves to a life of service, whether as a parent, as a schoolteacher, in political office, as a minister, in the army, or as a nurse. In the same way, the times when I have been happiest in my life have been those times when I have dedicated myself to helping others in whatever small ways I have been able to do so. Service animates the human spirit. It makes a person shine. Reminds us of our innate power to make a difference. Service affirms the dignity of a person and causes our spirits to soar. The happiest people I know are making a contribution.

Anyone who works with young people will tell you that

one of the biggest problems they face today is low self-esteem. As parents there are a great many things we can do to encourage self-esteem. This includes complimenting children when they make good decisions or act in ways that help them to become the-best-version-of-themselves. Sadly, when we compliment in our society we focus too much on what people look like and what people have. Self-esteem—a healthy sense of self—is not born from how we look or what we have, but rather from the innate ability to contribute and make a difference. If there is a self-esteem problem among young people today it is because we are failing to foster a spirit of service in their hearts.

How do we go about it? There are a thousand ways and most parents probably don't need to be told what they are. The simple ways my father modeled are commonplace enough for all of us to apply immediately. Beyond these everyday examples, volunteering at a homeless shelter or a soup kitchen, mowing a sick or elderly neighbor's lawn, visiting a nursing home, getting involved at church or in local politics are all things we can do with our children to help foster a spirit of service. In doing so, we make enormous contributions to their moral, ethical, and spiritual development. A couple of hours at a soup kitchen, however uncomfortable that may be, will do more for the moral, ethical, spiritual development of a child than a lifetime of Nintendo and MTV.

The earlier children learn to unleash their ability to contribute, the more abundant their experience of life will be.

Several months ago, as I walked away from the podium after speaking to several hundred leaders in the financial industry, the president of the organization pulled me aside and said, "Thanks, you really added value to our event today." What he said struck me. Every day people compliment me for giving great presentations, but his comments were unique because they drive to the very core of what we are here to do. Life is about adding value. Contribute or die is the law of the universe. In business, if we stop adding value it doesn't take long for the consequences to show themselves. But in society, it is all too easy to coast along without adding value, and worse yet, sponging from others what we need and want. How are we adding value? How are we teaching our children to add value? Not just to ourselves or to our bank balances, but to our family, our communities, our churches, our nation, and to humanity.

Foster a spirit of service in your children and you will find that long after you are gone it still serves them in their quest to discover self, contribute to society, and live a life of love, laughter, and happiness. Won't two people with a spirit of service have a better marriage than two without? Won't two neighbors with a spirit of service have a better friendship than two without? Won't two nations with a spirit of service make this a better world than two without?

Pray Together as a Family

Other than grace before meals and going to church on Sunday, my family never prayed together. When I speak of family prayer I am not speaking of grace before meals or going to church together on Sunday, but rather a time when a family gathers to pray together. It is something that had a place in a culture that now seems far off, but perhaps there is something that we can learn in our modern time from this old-fashioned ritual and practice.

Human beings have a spiritual side, or self. Most people acknowledge this. In fact, more than 92 percent of Americans, and more than 98 percent of the world's population, acknowledge that there is a God and that people have a spiritual capacity. Our understanding of God and the beliefs that surround that understanding may be many and varied, but the overwhelming majority of people can agree that there is a God and that we have a spiritual side to us.

In our present culture, there is an enormous struggle taking place around the way these issues should or should not affect public life. This debate includes the discussion of prayer in school, the role religion should play in politics, and so on. And yet, all of this seems peripheral to how we live and act in our personal lives.

As a parent, you may have very little influence over public policy, but you have enormous influence in your own home and in the lives of your children. If you are sincere in your quest to help your children grow free and strong to become the-best-version-of-themselves, I would encourage you to ask yourself: Will helping my children develop their spiritual self and senses help or hurt them in this quest?

Perhaps some will say it will hurt, but I would suggest that such an answer might be under the influence of biases and prejudices formed by exposure to the misuse and abuse of spirituality and religion rather than exposure to an authentic experience of the same.

I believe that family prayer has a powerful place in any family's culture. The form this prayer takes can, will, and should vary from one family to the next. I do not think there is one prescription that should be applied universally to this arena. I do believe that when we open ourselves to it, the Spirit will guide us as it does in all things.

Throughout my travels, I have seen many different families approach family prayer in many different ways. I have seen many families who do not engage in it at all. For the most part I would say that those families that do participate have better relationships than those that do not. This, of course, is a generalization. I have experienced families that pray together who are more dysfunctional than handfuls of families who do not pray together.

Sometimes family prayer doesn't work because of the format or the content, but most of the time it doesn't work because of the dictatorial way it is approached by certain parents and the way it is used to control and manipulate children. Aware that this happens and mindful that the abuse of a good does not necessarily diminish the goodness of something that is good, we press on.

Some parents will decide that they want to make prayer a part of their family culture, and others will decide that they don't. Depending on the ages of your children, I think you will meet with varying levels of resistance and success. If all of your children are under the age of ten, you have a very good chance of successfully implementing family prayer as part of your culture. The younger the children, the better your chances will be. If you have children between the ages of twelve and eighteen, your chances of success will be massively diminished depending on how consistent they see this practice as being part of the family culture in general.

Regardless, those of you who do decide you want to make family prayer a part of your culture, the questions you will most want to answer surround form and practice. There are a thousand ways this can be approached. I wish to share with you only one way here in this book. I think it will provide significant insight regardless of how you decide to approach family prayer. I have chosen this one in particular because I have found it to be simply the most effective method that I have been exposed to.

This is briefly how it works. A family gathers together one night during the week, perhaps on Tuesday or Wednesday for twenty to thirty minutes. It doesn't matter what night it is, but it does matter that it is the same night each week and at the same time. Give it a sacred place in your family's schedule.

When I first witnessed it, the father of this particular family read a short passage from the Bible. As it turned out, it was the reading that was going to be used the following Sunday at church, and this was done deliberately. After the reading, each member of the family was asked to comment briefly on a word or phrase or idea that jumped out at them from the reading. Then, the mother read the same reading aloud to everyone. Again, everyone was asked to comment on a word, phrase, or idea that struck him or her. Then, one of the children read the same reading a third time. Again, each person was invited to share something that touched them. "It can be the same thing each time or a different thing each time," the father explained to me.

It was quite extraordinary to see and hear children from five to sixteen openly sharing with one another what the Spirit was prompting within them.

Once this third round of sharing was over, the father asked if anyone had any intentions they would like the family to pray for this week. One of the children explained that his teacher was sick, another that her friend had lost her cat, and the mother explained that her friend's mother had died. One of the children then asked for prayers for his exams that week and another for success in a soccer competition in which she was competing. After several minutes of this, the mother led the family in a short formless spontaneous prayer, and their time of prayer was finished.

"Why is this so important?" I asked the parents later that night.

"So many ways," the wife replied. "It draws us out of ourselves and into one another's lives by making us aware of what is going on in the other's life. It demonstrates to the children that six people can hear the same passage and get six different messages. It helps them to develop spiritually by teaching them to listen to the voice of God in their lives. It teaches them that there is great value in being able to be still and quiet from time to time. I could go on and on. Of all the things we do to help our children grow up to be contributing members of the human family, this is perhaps the most important. There is enough structure to make it meaningful and manageable, but there is also enough room within the structure to be fully themselves. Isn't that how our experience of God and spirituality should always be?"

I was convinced. At the same time, if this has not been a

part of your family culture, I know how very difficult it is to implement. It may be hard enough to get your spouse to consent and participate, never mind the children. If you have very young children you are at a distinct advantage. Begin the practice now as a couple, and invite them to join you as they get older. In the meantime, have some version of family prayer on a regular basis. All that is needed is the right question: What should we pray for this week? You will be amazed by the answers you get from children only just old enough to talk. Children are often more in touch with the Spirit than we are. What is God saying to you this week? Again, you will be disarmed by some of the answers they give you. A simple question that everyone speaks to (especially the parents) and a short prayer is all it takes.

We may not agree about the role religion should play in the public life of our nation, we may not agree about which religion or form and practice of that religion is better than another. But surely we can agree that our children need better role models and leadership than the pop idols and icons of their age. Surely we can agree that helping them to develop spiritually will better equip them for life. We may differ in opinion surrounding form and practice, but in essence I think we can agree that someone who has had a chance to develop their spiritual self will approach life with an awareness that can be powerfully and practically applied to every arena of life.

Raising amazing children is a full-time job. If it was the only thing you had to do, you would still not have enough time to do it to the best of your abilities. Parenting, like most things in life, is about making the best of limited resources. You do the best you can with what you have where you are. There are no perfect parents, but some are better than others. The best ones are dedicated to continuous improvement. They don't read a book about parenting and make it their Bible on the subject. They read many books about parenting, history, business, relationships, and any other number of subjects. They talk to friends at work, at school, and at church. They listen to audiobooks and attend seminars both personally and professionally. They see movies and listen to music. They eat and exercise and make love. In short, they live their lives. And as they do, they pause after daily experiences and ask themselves: What did I learn from this that can make me a better parent to my children?

5

The Future of the World Passes by Way of the Family

In the past, politicians would speak to the people of their nations about building a great society. The speeches of Franklin Delano Roosevelt, Abraham Lincoln, and Winston Churchill are filled with descriptions of what constitutes a great society and how they wanted to lead their nations in the building of the great societies they envisioned. Each lived in a different time, and yet each urged their people to reach farther.

Today we talk much more about preserving our great societies. The underlying assumption, of course, is that we have great societies to preserve. It is that assumption that I think we need to question. If the assumption is true, then it will hold up to our questioning. If the assumption is false, then we will all be better off for being ushered into the light of truth however harsh that light may be. Then, armed with this new knowledge, we will be awakened to the task that is before us.

I do not doubt that we have made advances in the past hundred years in the areas of science, technology, and finance. These advances have been incredible. However, if we consider what our children have to face every day at school, in society, and in many cases at home, I think a cloud of doubt begins to gather over our great society assumption.

Surely, a truly great society would not submit their children to so many of the situations and circumstances our children face on a daily basis?

The danger here is that while we are all eating, drinking, and being merry in the shadow of such a false assumption, nobody is out working to make what we have falsely assumed to be real, a reality. It isn't until someone stands up and says "We have a problem!" that the great minds of our generation will begin seeking out and implementing the solution.

Friends and Enemies

In Chapter 2 we discussed the idea that we are in the midst of a cultural war and that our children are the targets. In preparing to write this book, I shared this idea with many people to gauge their reactions. Usually they would give me strange looks or they would look away not knowing what to say. I sensed that they were thinking that I was a bit extreme, so I called them on it. Most of them admitted that that was what they were thinking. But then I started talking to them about what they hoped for their children and what their children were up against in society today, and little by little I could see the realization awakening in their eyes.

I believe you picked up this book, and have read this far into it, because you are dedicated to some or all of the following:

- Building a better family
- Raising amazing children

- Having a great marriage
- Becoming the-best-version-of-yourself

I think some of what has filled these pages may have come as a surprise to many parents. But I also think that we have simply become immune to most of it in ways that is hurting our children and damaging our judgment as parents. Most of all, I think it becomes abundantly clear that if we genuinely want to achieve the things listed above we have friends and enemies in that effort. And the fact that you find yourself surrounded by friends and enemies in your quest to raise your children means that you are in the midst of a war. The question is: Who are your friends and who are your enemies?

We discussed the five things that are critical to know in order to win a war.

1. That you *are* at war
2. What you are fighting for, who and what you are defending, why it is important to win, and what is at stake if you lose
3. Who your allies are
4. Who or what your enemy is, and
5. What weapons and strategies can defeat your enemies

Throughout this book we have addressed each of these five points. It is my hope that it has become abundantly clear that: you are at war; you are fighting for and defending your family, your children, your marriage, and the-best-version-of-yourself; your allies are character and virtue, and any per-

son, program, or institution that celebrates these; your enemies are complacency, apathy, ignorance, many forms of
modern technology (though they need not be), many forms
of modern entertainment, often the modern media, and the
status quo. The weapons and strategies you can employ to
defeat these enemies are too many to list here as they have
been the subject of the bulk of this book.

The mere fact that you now realize that you are in the
midst of a war will change the way you live and act and
speak as a parent. The greatest downfall of not realizing that
we are at war is that we mistake our enemies for friends. In
The Art of War, Sun Tzu discusses the importance of knowing one's enemy. The insights in this text have been applied to
modern business and certainly to the realm of professional
sports. Every day, coaches study tape of the coming weekend's opponents in an attempt to know the way their oppo-
nent will respond in certain situations. I suspect it is high
time that we apply this wisdom to parenting.

If, as a parent, your goal is to raise amazing children who
can go out into the world and celebrate the-best-version-of-
themselves, you need to consider who your opponents are in
this quest. You also need to think long and hard about who
your friends and allies are in this war. Sadly, in your search
for friends and allies, you will come up with a much shorter
list than your list of enemies and detractors. That alone
should give you pause to reflect.

One of your greatest allies is simplicity. Raising children is
at once difficult, complex, and simple. At one level it is as
simple as spending time with them, listening to them, and let-

ting them know that they are loved. On another level the complications of modern life—the demands placed on our time in the workplace, the challenges related to finances, and the pressure that all of this brings to bear on ourselves and our relationships—makes raising children perhaps more complex than at any other time in history.

If you read the writings of the great minds of every generation or study their lives and their work, you will find a common thread. They believe that beauty, truth, genius, and power is hidden in simplicity. Da Vinci, Michelangelo, Galileo, Edison, Einstein . . . all extolled the virtues of simplicity. They believed that behind all the complexity there is a simple answer to the most complex problems, and it is that simple answer that they sought. Business leaders today are searching constantly to apply this wisdom to their various endeavors. Those who rise to the top in almost any field are those who are able to break down the most complex situations and problems into a series of simple solutions. Success as a parent depends on you finding a model of simplicity and applying it to your life and the life of your family. In so doing, you will give your children not only the peace and joy that flows from experiencing simplicity, but also a blueprint for their lives.

If you picked up this book hoping that I would give you a list of ten things to do as a parent, you are by now sorely disappointed. I don't apologize, but encourage you to put your own list together. I have shared in this book dozens and dozens of ideas. From all of them, select three or four. Write them down. Commit yourself to implementing them into your life and your family's culture. Once you have firmly established them as habits, return to this book, read it again, and select three or four more.

Allow nothing to overwhelm you, take each day on its merits, and never let a day pass without pausing to recognize that the life of your child is a miracle.

As we have explored these topics, it has become abundantly clear that as a parent you need allies. Children need the time and energy of loving parents, but they also need mentors, coaches, teachers, siblings, and friends to challenge and encourage them to seek out the-best-version-of-themselves. They need environments that allow them to grow, discover themselves, and thrive. All of these provide worthy allies.

At first it may seem as if you don't have many allies in your quest to raise amazing children and build a dynamic environment, but that may be because you have not been looking for them. Now that you are aware of their role and your need for them, they will begin to emerge in your daily life and you will begin to engage them as strategic partners.

Looking into the Future

The future passes by way of the family. Every man and woman on this planet has been influenced for better or worse by the family he or she was born into. It is an influence that we still do not quite understand and it is an influence that is inescapable. Children whose mothers abandoned them at birth spend their whole lives trying to understand how that may have affected them. Children whose mothers give them up for adoption do the same. Children born into loving families where the father or mother works too much visit therapists every day trying to understand the inexplicable. The examples and stories are endless. Families have an enormous influence on our lives.

Beyond the personal impact our family circumstances have on us, sooner or later we need to step back as a society and ask ourselves: What impact is our family culture having on our future as a society and nation?

Take the most common and well-know statistic of our time: 50 percent of marriages end in divorce or separation. How is this one aspect of our modern culture affecting our society and nation? The implications and repercussions are too many and numerous to explore here, but I think the average person on the street can probably see that the effect of such a cultural phenomena is not good for individuals, families, society, or our nation.

Family is a deeply personal experience, but it is one that echoes throughout our lives and down through history. Raising children is a deeply personal endeavor, but it is one that sends waves of love or hatred, virtue or vice, selfishness or generosity down through history.

If we glance through the looking glass we call family, we can see clearly what the future of our society and nation looks like. I suspect it is a vision that most of us would like to improve upon.

If we truly wish to build a great modern society, do we actually believe we can do so without restoring the dignity and the unity of the family? If our delusion runs this deep, then I will grow even more concerned for our children and those of generations to come. But I have hope. I believe the tide is turning. I meet people every day who are working toward making this world a place where their children can grow free and strong, unencumbered by the marks of despotism that too many of our children are forced to deal with too young in their lives.

The family is the cornerstone of all great societies. Anyone who wishes to play any role in shaping the future should focus his or her efforts here. It is time for the great minds of our generation to start imagining a great renaissance of family life. It is time to present a vision of family that we can all celebrate as good and true, noble and beautiful, regardless of our own history with the idea of family.

Family is both deeply personal and monumentally historic. The future of the world passes by way of the family.

Epilogue

There are two documents on the wall of the dining room of our family home in Sydney. They have been there for as long as I can remember, and on several occasions over the past thirty years or so, I have paused to reflect upon them. I would like to share them with you now. The first is easy to read and difficult to live. It speaks to our responsibilities as parents. The second is more difficult to read and just as difficult to live. It speaks to our responsibilities as human beings.

Children Learn What They Live

By Dorothy Law Nolte

If a child lives with criticism,
 He learns to condemn.
If a child lives with hostility,
 He learns to fight.
If a child lives with ridicule,
 He learns to be shy.
If a child lives with shame,
 He learns to feel guilty.
If a child lives with tolerance,
 He learns to be patient.
If a child lives with encouragement,
 He learns confidence.
If a child lives with praise,
 He learns to appreciate.
If a child lives with fairness,
 He learns justice.
If a child lives with security,
 He learns to have faith.
If a child lives with approval,
 He learns to like himself.
If a child lives with acceptance and friendship,
 He learns to find love in the world.

Declaration of the Rights of the Child

WHEREAS the peoples of the United Nations have, in the Charter, reaffirmed their faith in fundamental human rights and in the dignity and worth of the human person, and have determined to promote social progress and better standards of life in larger freedom,

WHEREAS the United Nations has, in the Universal Declaration of Human Rights, proclaimed that everyone is entitled to all the rights and freedoms set forth therein, without distinction of any kind, such as race, colour, sex, language, religion, political or other opinion, national or social origin, property, birth or other status,

WHEREAS the child, by reason of his physical and mental immaturity, needs special safeguards and care, including appropriate legal protection, before as well as after birth,

WHEREAS the need for such special safeguards has been stated in the Geneva Declaration of the Rights of the Child of 1924, and recognized in the Universal Declaration of Human Rights and in the statutes of specialized agencies and international organizations concerned with the welfare of children,

WHEREAS mankind owes to the child the best it has to give,

NOW THEREFORE, THE GENERAL ASSEMBLY PRO-
CLAIMS this Declaration of the Rights of the Child to
the end that he may have a happy childhood and enjoy
for his own good and for the good of society the rights
and freedoms herein set forth, and calls upon parents,
upon men and women as individuals, and upon volun-
tary organizations, local authorities and national Gov-
ernments to recognize these rights and strive for their
observance by legislative and other measures progres-
sively taken in accordance with the following principles:

PRINCIPLE 1

The child shall enjoy all the rights set forth in this Declaration. Every child, without any exception whatso-
ever, shall be entitled to these rights, without distinction
or discrimination on account of race, colour, sex, language, religion, political or other opinion, national or
social origin, property, birth or other status, whether of
himself or of his family.

PRINCIPLE 2

The child shall enjoy special protection, and shall be
given opportunities and facilities, by law and by other
means, to enable him to develop physically, mentally,
morally, spiritually and socially in a healthy and normal
manner and in conditions of freedom and dignity. In the
enactment of laws for this purpose, the best interests of
the child shall be the paramount consideration.

PRINCIPLE 3

The child shall be entitled from his birth to a name and a nationality.

PRINCIPLE 4

The child shall enjoy the benefits of social security. He shall be entitled to grow and develop in health; to this end, special care and protection shall be provided both to him and to his mother, including adequate pre-natal and post-natal care. The child shall have the right to adequate nutrition, housing, recreation and medical services.

PRINCIPLE 5

The child who is physically, mentally or socially handicapped shall be given the special treatment, education and care required by his particular condition.

PRINCIPLE 6

The child, for the full and harmonious development of his personality, needs love and understanding. He shall, wherever possible, grow up in the care and under the responsibility of his parents, and, in any case, in an atmosphere of affection and of moral and material security; a child of tender years shall not, save in exceptional circumstances, be separated from his mother. Society and the public authorities shall have the duty to extend particular care to children without a family and to those without adequate means of support. Payment of State and other assistance toward the maintenance of children of large families is desirable.

PRINCIPLE 7

The child is entitled to receive education, which shall be free and compulsory, at least in the elementary stages. He shall be given an education which will promote his general culture and enable him, on a basis of equal opportunity, to develop his abilities, his individual judgment, and his sense of moral and social responsibility, and to become a useful member of society.

The best interests of the child shall be the guiding principle of those responsible for his education and guidance; that responsibility lies in the first place with his parents.

The child shall have full opportunity for play and recreation, which should be directed to the same purposes as education; society and the public authorities shall endeavor to promote the enjoyment of this right.

PRINCIPLE 8

The child shall in all circumstances be among the first to receive protection and relief.

PRINCIPLE 9

The child shall be protected against all forms of neglect, cruelty and exploitation. He shall not be the subject of traffic, in any form.

The child shall not be admitted to employment before an appropriate minimum age; he shall in no case be caused or permitted to engage in any occupation or employment which would prejudice his health or education, or interfere with his physical, mental or moral development.

PRINCIPLE 10

The child shall be protected from practices which may foster racial, religious and any other form of discrimination. He shall be brought up in a spirit of understanding, tolerance, friendship among peoples, peace and universal brotherhood, and in full consciousness that his energy and talents should be devoted to the service of his fellow men.

Proclaimed by General Assembly resolution 1386(XIV) of 20 November 1959.

I once asked my father why he and my mother had chosen to hang these on the wall in our home. He told me that first and foremost they were there for him and not for my brothers and me. He explained that they were there to remind him of the privilege and responsibilities of being a parent. We talked for a long time then about many things. I can still hear his voice . . .

"We wanted you to see that we have a vision for the type of environment we want you to grow up in, and remind ourselves because at times we all lose sight of what matters most.

"I wanted you and your brothers to know that you have rights, that you are entitled to be treated with a certain respect and dignity. Not because you are my children and not because of anything you have accomplished or achieved, but simply because you are human beings.

"Your mother and I wanted you to learn early in life that rights are not to be taken lightly and never to be used as an excuse for cheap thrills.

"Whenever you go to other places and encounter other people in this world, whether it be school or a foreign land, remember that you have rights, but also that others have the right to be treated fairly and with decency.

"Matthew, the UN has declared these things, but people are people—capable of great love and capable of great selfishness. Never forget that there are a great many children in this world who are denied these rights every day of their lives.

"Be grateful for who you are and all you have, and do what you can to make this world a better place for those who cross your path, especially children who are less fortunate than yourself. You cannot do anything for children in Africa or Asia, but there are children in your class at school who have real heartaches and challenges that you will never know. Be kind to them, include them, we all need to know that we are loved."

By now it was abundantly clear that my mother and father had not just framed these pieces and thrown them on the wall because they looked good. They had a vision of what parenting and family were all about. How did they do? Amazingly well, I think. My brothers and I have no doubt betrayed their vision from time to time and in doing so have brought heartache upon ourselves and our family. My parents gave us a foundation for life, where we have taken it from there and will take it in the future is entirely up to us. Were they perfect parents? No, certainly not, and they would be the first to admit it. They would tell you that they did the best they knew how at the time. Can any more be expected of a parent? I think not. To make parenting a priority and keep trying to improve, this is the great commission of a parent.

About the Author

MATTHEW KELLY is the author of several books, including *Perfectly Yourself, The Rhythm of Life, The Seven Levels of Intimacy,* and *The Dream Manager.* His books have appeared on multiple bestseller lists, including those of *The New York Times, USA Today,* and *The Wall Street Journal.* For more than a decade Kelly has been traveling the globe, and more than three million people in fifty countries have attended his seminars. Kelly is the founder of The Matthew Kelly Foundation, whose major charitable work is to help young people discover their mission in life. Kelly is also the president of Floyd Consulting, a Chicago-based consulting company that helps corporations become the-best-version-of-themselves.